ADVANCE PRAISE FOR *Living with the Enemy*

"I have had the privilege and—at times—the challenge of hearing the stories of a number of extraordinary people. I am heartened to read how Burt Nordstrand has put his life and achievements into perspective. He demonstrates that healthy recovery from an eating disorder is achievable."

—*Mike Schiks, executive director, Project Turnabout Addiction Recovery Center, former executive vice president of Hazelden Treatment Services for 21 years.*

"Burt Nordstrand is a pioneer and a successful entrepreneur who has been a major contributor to the health and future of Hudson, Wisconsin, and other communities. I admire his passion, creativity and perseverance, but mostly his honesty and his commitment to his family, friends and community."

—*Ken Heiser, president of First National Bank of Hudson, Wisconsin, for 28 years.*

Danielle
With Gratitude
Burt Nordstrand

LIVING
WITH
THE
ENEMY

AN EXPLORATION OF
ADDICTION & RECOVERY

BURT NORDSTRAND with CAROL PINE

BEAVER'S
POND
PRESS

Portions of the 12 Steps of Alcoholics Anonymous are from *Alcoholics Anonymous:
Big Book*, Fourth Edition, Alcoholics Anonymous World Services, Inc., 2001.

Portions of the 12 Steps of Overeaters Anonymous are from *Overeaters Anonymous*,
Overeaters Anonymous, Inc., 1980.

Cover photographs by Chadd Ziegler

ISBN 10: 1-59298-336-7
ISBN 13: 978-1-59298-336-0

Library of Congress Catalog Number: 2010927022

Printed in the United States of America

Second Printing: 2012

16 15 14 13 12   5 4 3 2

Cover and interior design by James Monroe Design, LLC.

BEAVER'S
POND
PRESS

Beaver's Pond Press, Inc.
7104 Ohms Lane, Suite 101
Edina, MN 55439–2129
(952) 829-8818
www.BeaversPondPress.com

To order, visit www.BeaversPondBooks.com
or call (800) 901-3480. Reseller discounts available.

TO MY GRANDCHILDREN, WITH LOVE

Nicholas Burton
Samuel David
Isaac Thomas
Michael Matthew
Seth Lee
Sonny John
Murphy Carolyn
Samara Sky
John (Jack) Robert

And those yet to come

**The adventures you dream are the life you will live.
Life is short. Go for it!**

CONTENTS

A WORD FROM THE AUTHOR

This is my story—my remembrances of the events of my life. These recollections are my own. Others may remember things differently, but any misrepresentation or misinterpretation on my part was unintentional.

FOREWORD

For most of his life, Burt Nordstrand was the quintessential entrepreneur with a vision and drive that made nearly everything he touched a success. Yet, in spite of all his external accomplishments and public adulation, Burt had a disabling secret, his multiple addictions that were fueled by an overwhelming sense of insecurity and unworthiness. The "hole" in his soul could not be filled by chemicals, gambling, sex, or food.

This book chronicles his pain and quiet desperation with heartfelt honesty. In particular, he captures the destructive power and emotional turmoil caused by compulsive overeating, a serious illness that is seldomly acknowledged by men.

This is a story of recovery from multiple addictions to a life in balance, a wonderfully detailed and grace-filled journey home, to a life filled with peace and serenity. Burt beautifully illustrates the important relationships in his life that carried him through an amazing transformation to wellness. He makes the 12-Step program come alive as the foundation of a life well lived. Burt Nordstrand's message is one of hope and healing that will touch anyone who has suffered from multiple addictions and is seeking the grace of a whole life recovery.

John H. Curtiss, M.A., LADC, NCRS
*President and co-founder of The Retreat, a chemical dependency
recovery center in Wayzata, Minnesota, and
former Hazelden Foundation executive for 19 years.*

ACKNOWLEDGMENTS

My thanks to the people who made this life possible: the team at SSG Corporation and BNA, real estate partners and other associates—including Gail Nordstrand Dahlstrom, Scott Nordstrand, Ron Nordstrand, Dennis Nordstrand, Bill Wanner, Kathy Ostlund, Larry Hopkins, Sue Kenall Zappa, Larry Mitchell, Tom Reeck, Carrie Monnot, Don Campbell, Steve Wellington, Kevin Vance, Deno Sotos, and Jeff Tegeler.

I also thank my friends who helped with this book and have kept me balanced, whether skiing on the slopes, hiking up Vail Mountain, sailing in the Caribbean, taking bike trips, or simply being there for me: John Peterson, Neil McGraw, Jerry McGraw, Hermann Staufer, Dan Burns, Peter Vogt, Tim Forsythe, Steve Kluz, Matt Forsgren, and many others. Thanks to editor Marly Cornell, designer James Monroe, the folks at Beaver's Pond Press, readers and editors Scott Nordstrand, Tom Horner, Tim and Mary Forsythe, and Mike Schiks.

Special thanks to my family—especially Yvonne—who listens kindly to "the world according to Burt."

Over the years, my friends and I often sat in the cockpit of my sailboat early in the morning, sharing and reflecting on the stories of our lives that could have been episodes in a book. I did not seriously consider actually writing a book about my life until I realized that I wanted my children and grandchildren—who in all likelihood will benefit from my financial success—to know about the struggles and joys of my life and the important lessons I have learned, in some cases, the hard way.

With some research and a little bit of luck, I found my writing partner and co-author, Carol Pine. This project would not have happened without her. I made the decision to work with her after a telephone call with my friend Tom Horner. When I called Carol, she said she'd love to do it, but she was busy for a year. I said, "No problem, I can wait." The following year, after a couple of interviews, we made arrangements to meet on my sailboat, *Serenity*, in the Caribbean. Carol is also an accomplished sailor as well as a writer. For one week, armed with a simple timeline, I spent sixty hours telling her my story. We had the tapes transcribed and that was the beginning.

Only when this book began to take shape did I realize that sharing my life experiences with a broader audience might have the additional potential to help others who have known some of the same struggles. I wish you smooth sailing.

*Life shrinks or expands
in proportion to one's courage.*
—Anais Nin

PREFACE

This is my story—a story about a man who was emotionally scarred, beginning as a child. At an early age, I discovered that sugar changed the way I felt. Sugar made me feel more "normal." From that point on, I did whatever I had to do to maintain that feeling: more sugar, compulsive overeating, speed (diet pills), nicotine, caffeine, alcohol, undisciplined and irresponsible sex, and projects sometimes undertaken with the goal of winning adulation. All these worked for a time—some longer than others.

I built a business from virtually nothing, pushed myself hard, and moved at warp speed. I was proud of my stamina, control, and penchant for perfection. The excitement, drama, and gambles of entrepreneurial life thrilled me. The very qualities that defined me as an addict also made me a successful entrepreneur. In fact, the qualities that define entrepreneurs and addicts are remarkably similar. Age forty left me with compulsive overeating, controlling my weight with bulimic behavior, and over-exercising. All the while I compulsively pursued my business ventures with considerable success.

Like a growing number of Americans suffering with addiction, I had what people often call "a high bottom." I could still function in the world and—on the surface—my life appeared charmed. I even looked healthy and strong. Inside, however, I was crumbling, and my personal life suffered. I hit my "bottom" when, for all appearances, I was fit and happy. I knew the *real* truth. I couldn't live a double life of outward success and inward devastation any longer. This "bottom" led me to recovery.

Age fifty found me working a successful 12-Step program and beginning to discover the miracle of recovery. By continuing to "work" my program of recovery, I came to realize that giving up being in charge of everything, and turning my life over to a power greater than myself, brought serenity and peace of mind.

But, I still have to "live with the enemy"—food.

ONE

RURAL ROOTS WITH
A SUGAR HIGH

AN OCEAN INVENTORY: 2008

Three A.M. and my senses are on high alert. The only sound is water racing along the slick, fiberglass hull as my sailboat carves the waves. Starlight shines on the water's surface, and a full moon cuts a liquid path across the Caribbean between Dominica and St. Lucia.

I'm alone in the cockpit. I see more stars from here than anyone can see on land. In a couple hours, I'll spot a faint, amber glow on the eastern horizon. Dawn. Maybe even a visit from curious dolphins as the sun comes up.

Until then, it's me, the huge ocean and my boat—its sails drawing power from the trade winds. Occasional, faint navigation lights shine from distant ships and buoys. The lighted compass shows the course I've charted. An autopilot steers *Serenity*, my fifty-four-foot Hylas sloop.

For a sailor, the cockpit at night is an opportunity for reflection.

Hours will pass before my two mates wake for their watch. I have the luxury of fair, warm winds and time without land-based distractions. No cell, PDA, TV. No chatter. Nothing.

I am seventy years old. I am fit and strong enough to ski all day in the back bowls of Vail, hike 14,000-foot mountains in Colorado, bike Mount Evans (the highest paved road in North America), and swim a half mile in these warm, tropical waters. I'm in recovery from prostate cancer. I am blessed with a loving partner, Yvonne, and a large, blended family of siblings, sons, daughters, and grandchildren. My business is more successful and satisfying than I ever dreamed, and my colleagues keep it humming day to day. Though I'm often out of town, I'm never out of touch. I spend a third of my time on this boat, another third in Vail, and the balance in St. Paul, Florida, and on a major international trip each year. It's a dream life.

Because of my material success, I can now imagine more meaningful ways to give back personally and financially. I lost six million dollars—perhaps more—in America's recent economic melt-down, but it doesn't scare me. I no longer equate net worth with self-worth.

I feel overpowering gratitude, and the tears come. To look at my life today, you might think I was always one of the lucky ones—a golden boy with all the benefits, traveling the easy, uncluttered road to the destination I chose.

Anything but. I would be long dead had I kept the life course I charted early on. My legacy would have read like this:

broken marriages; loneliness; lost opportunities; self-will run riot; unbridled fear; obesity; hopeless addiction to food, caffeine, alcohol, prescription pills, gambling, and work; a highly capable con artist, mired in self-loathing; and an opportunistic egomaniac with a deep inferiority complex.

I changed course about twenty-eight years ago. I finally asked for help. I gave up living a double life of outward success and inner turmoil. If I could save my own life with this pack of addictions and struggles, which still lives with me today, anyone can. What I understand now—that I did not fully appreciate then—is simple: I *never* did it alone.

THE OUTLIER

As a kid growing up on a farm in rural Ellsworth, Wisconsin, I was often sad and lonesome, chunky from my earliest days, a goof-off who gravitated to sugar and to lost people who were nursing their own private miseries. I was the underachiever of four children whose parents always provided a safe home with food on the table and more comforts than most rural farms enjoyed in the 1940s and '50s.

Though our home was comfortable, lingering fear—like a heavy fog—enveloped our little world. Dad feared poor crops and financial disaster. The polio scare of the 1950s seized our small town, and all of us feared being paralyzed and trapped in an iron lung. The Cold War between America and Russia had us practicing emergency drills in our basement bomb shelters—a fixture in many homes of the era.

Our house was the center of a little universe of working farms, the place where neighbors gathered for Christmas, camaraderie, gossip, and talk of farm futures, fertilizer, and livestock feed. A half mile away, our little church, the Swedish Covenant Mission, served up its brand of fundamental Protestantism. No Catholics lived in my neighborhood, which covered about two square miles. *They* didn't venture in, and *we* didn't venture out. Almost like growing up on a block in the Bronx or Brooklyn, there you stayed.

We walked about a mile through the local cemetery and farm

fields to reach our one-room school. My older brother, Dennis, was usually frustrated because I lagged about a hundred yards behind him and dawdled. He pulled me by the arm to get me going. When we arrived in winter, the school was frigid and we went to work lighting the wood stove. The whole student body—about ten of us in grades one through twelve—huddled around that stove for morning lessons. Of course, by afternoon we were cooking. A trip to the school's outhouse cooled us off.

Dirt roads led to downtown Ellsworth, a homely collection of merchants that included a grocery store, The Spot ice cream shop, creamery, feed mill, gas station, and several shadowy, beer-infused bars: Most's; Snowball's; and the roadside Triangle Tavern, a popular destination on the way home from town. I hung out there with my older neighbors who bought me candy bars and Coke while they drank—an almost daily ritual.

USING PALS

Edgar Holden was one of those people. He was a loveable giant, probably six feet, six inches and three hundred pounds, who lived with his mother and brother across the road from us. When his mother died and his brother married and moved away, Edgar stayed in that little house as it slowly decayed. I remember fires in his kitchen and outdoor toilet. He simply shut off the smoldering, sooty rooms and moved into the next one, using a hot plate for his galley and a pail for his toilet. He was dirt poor.

Edgar bathed every few weeks and wore grimy coveralls. He often visited our home and, if he didn't pick an especially sturdy chair, he broke furniture with his bulk.

Edgar was a smart guy who taught my parents a lot about farming. He knew how to get things done, and he was generous with his time and attention. Edgar took me places my parents didn't have time for, like fishing; and he was patient with my boyish questions.

But Edgar was "different." As best I can describe Edgar, he was a hermaphrodite; he had the qualities of both sexes buried in one body. I distinctly remember that he never had to shave. As a kid of seven, I went to the tavern with Edgar many afternoons after finishing farm chores. He'd drink himself into a stupor while playing, and often winning, card games. I wonder now if his sexual confusion fueled his drinking.

Though he was a father figure and role model for me, Edgar's drinking scared me and so did his confusing sexuality. I worried that I might grow up like him: alcoholic, not fully a man. Amazingly, Edgar died of old age at eighty, in spite of his lifelong heavy drinking.

There were also Vernon Johnson, a hired hand down the street, and Les Clobes, a bachelor, who lived with his brother and worked a nearby farm. As I got older, I often pretended to go to school, but instead turned up with Edgar, Vernon, or Les down at the taverns. They bought me soft drinks or ice cream, feeding my budding sugar addiction, and they drank like the alcoholics they were. No one—not even my parents—seemed to notice.

I gravitated to the oddballs. Marion and Everett Anderson, our nearest neighbors, were kind-hearted and generous people. But Everett's brother Verne was a bachelor who lived upstairs in their home and quietly hoarded every penny he earned. He was like the other older guys I hung around with—quirky, disconnected loners. I wanted to be around them. I saw some of myself in them. They were all addicts. This was my neighborhood and, looking back, my entire world was dysfunctional.

My bachelor farmer friends had particular views, especially about women, which I adopted by association. Women were objects, lesser beings, sneaky manipulators. They wanted to take over our lives, but all they were really good for was sex. Women were the enemy.

I don't know why the older guys took me under their wings. I tried to be nice and funny and likeable. I had already learned to charm and manipulate them to get ice cream and candy bars. I guess I was entertainment, a diversion, and I helped them home after long afternoons of drinking. Surprisingly, there was no overt sexual abuse. I wanted so much to be liked; I would have been an easy mark for any one of them.

Donald Stockwell was the only close friend I had who was my same age. He came from a family that lived nearby. I didn't pal around with my brothers. Dennis, the oldest, and my younger brother, Ron, were the conscientious kids in the Nordstrand family.

When our sister Gail was born, she fit that mold, too. I was the "outlier," the kid with a learning disability who made up for his deficiencies with street smarts. My big brother, Dennis, told me I was a goof-off loudly and often. If the shoe fits, I guessed, wear it to the hilt.

THE SWEDISH INVASION

My ancestors were all hardworking Swedes who struggled to realize the American Dream. Many years passed before I discovered I had the same instincts buried under pounds of fat and insecurity.

All four of my grandparents, along with several of their siblings, were part of the huge wave of Swedish immigrants who came to the United States in the late 1800s and early 1900s. They shared their stories with us. All of them sought land and new opportunities because they had lost hope at home. Swedish family farms had been divided so many times among the sons in each large family that only tiny farms remained. The farms were so meager; they couldn't support even one family.

Swedes in their homeland heard about the golden promise of America and a flood of immigration took them by train to Gothenburg, where they sailed to the east coast of England. From there, another train carried them across England to Liverpool or Glasgow. Their final leg was the rugged ocean crossing to New York Harbor where—if they survived the crossing—they joined countless thousands from many countries, waiting to pass inspection at Ellis Island. The criminals were not the only ones turned away. It was also the sick and mentally ill.

Many Swedes took trains to Chicago, and some continued on to Iowa, Wisconsin, and Minnesota. My ancestors settled in "Swede Town"—a collection of houses, apartments, churches, clubs, schools, and even newspapers—right in the center of Chicago. A Swede could live and die there without ever speaking another language.

Swedish men worked as underpaid laborers, and girls and women became maids or joined sweatshops where the hours were long, the pay pitiful, and the conditions deplorable. Some lucky Swedes with skills joined the building trades. One of those was my paternal grandfather, Hjalmar Nordstrand, an accomplished carpenter and construction superintendent.

Grandpa Nordstrand and men like him were nicknamed the "Swedes that built Chicago" because they showed up, demonstrated surprising craftsmanship and toughness, put in a full day's work, and never let you down.

My grandpa was single when he immigrated to America in 1900 and became a citizen in 1906 at twenty-three. He met Olga, eighteen, a tall, blue-eyed brunette with a strong will, and married her two years later. Olga had arrived in Chicago in 1902.

The groom had advantages: he could read, write, and speak English. He worked as a house carpenter and even owned his own home, with a mortgage. He and Grandma welcomed their first son, Arthur, in 1910 and my father, Alvin, one year later in 1911. Dad had an impressive name bigger than he was: Alvin Hjalmar Immanuel Nordstrand. But work wasn't steady in those days, even for a skilled carpenter. The family gave up their home in Chicago, and just before World War I ended in 1918, Grandma made their home in a tiny farmhouse in Pierce County, Wisconsin, while Grandpa worked in the city. But the experiment in rural life failed. One more time, the Nordstrand family put down roots in Chicago. They rented a house for sixty-five dollars a month on Spaulding Avenue around 1928, just one year before an economic meltdown burned America.

THE HORSE WHISPERER

My mom's father, Charles Swanson, arrived in Galesburg, Illinois, from Westergotland, Sweden, more than a decade before Grandpa Nordstrand landed in Chicago. The little town in Northwest Illinois, fifty miles east of the Mississippi River, was a haven for Swedes; and Grandpa Swanson, then twenty-two, settled with his cousin. Counting on promises of help, Grandpa was instead treated more like a slave than family. To survive, he stole milk from the family cow and ate fresh eggs from under their laying hens. He soon landed a sales job with Armour and Company, the well-known meat packer, in Galesburg.

Seven years after he arrived in 1888, my much-older Grandpa Swanson met Ida Swanson, a sixteen-year-old Swedish immigrant, and married her. The couple had two daughters, Esther and Ruth, and made their life in Galesburg for twelve years before they packed up and traveled west to Sumner, Nebraska, with a new plan. Grandpa rented a ranch and took up horse training. No one knows if Grandpa had the skills to be a horse whisperer, but he chose a prosperous farm community where his countrymen settled and might take a chance on him. There, in the tiny, south central Nebraska town, my mom, Helen, was born in 1912.

Mom bloomed on the ranch. She loved animals and gravitated to the horses. One day, the family lost track of her, only to find little Helen cozied up in the barn with a hefty horse restrained in a stanchion. At any moment, that horse could have killed her with a flying hoof, but mom had no fear. At only five years old, her parents bought her a Shetland pony and carried the squirming pet home in the backseat of their car. Mom trained that unruly pony well and spent countless hours riding the Nebraska range.

Mom was only about six years old when her mother, Ida, died in a worldwide flu epidemic that claimed twenty-two million lives between 1918 and 1920. Mom's father, my Grandpa Charles, was heartbroken and seemed incapable of raising his youngest daughter alone. He entrusted her upbringing to Mom's oldest sister, Esther, newly married in Nebraska, and her aunt, Helen, in Chicago.

Mom was lonely and confused as a little girl. She told me years later, "I didn't know who I belonged to in those years." But all that changed when her father returned to Sweden in 1920. He met Olga Zetterlund, the manager of a local meat market and, within eight months of Grandpa Charles' return to America, Olga landed in New York City. The couple settled in a predominantly Jewish neighborhood of Chicago on Ainslie Street, and Olga became Helen's doting stepmother. Helen was rewarded with a baby sister, too. Constance was born in 1922.

WOOING OUTSIDE WOOLWORTH

Mom's family had it hard. Her father worked as a wholesale fruit salesman, and they rented their home for forty-five dollars a week. By the time Mom was in ninth grade, her family needed help. She left school and found a job working for eleven cents an hour as a saleslady at F.W. Woolworth, the first five-and-dime store in America. At sixteen, working ten hours a day, she helped cover the family rent. After four years on the job, Mom was promoted to head cashier at Woolworth's newest store on Chicago's North Side. She took home forty dollars a week.

On a Sunday night in 1928 Mom attended Luther League at her church and met Alvin Nordstrand, my father. He went with his cousin Burt who promised the meeting was a great place to meet girls you could actually bring home to Mother. Alvin had graduated from high school, and he was learning to be a carpenter, just like his dad. He wanted a wife.

Dad was smitten from the start, but Mom was leery. She wasn't even neutral; she didn't like Alvin Nordstrand. She turned him down for dates and waited to see how long he persevered. When Dad made a practice of meeting her outside Woolworth's on the nights she worked late, Mom's resistance softened. He walked her safely home, and Grandma Swanson usually had a treat waiting for them. Mom finally consented to a *real* date, and Dad impressed her with his frugality: if they got to the theater before 6:30 P.M., they only paid a dime each.

THE FIRST MELT DOWN

The go-go years of the 1920s—filled with optimism, stock market fireworks, and a lot of dirty dealing on Wall Street—came to a screeching halt on Black Tuesday, October 29, 1929. On that day, the U.S. stock market imploded and a world economic crisis began. U.S. securities lost $30 billion in value that week—a catastrophe never imagined by even the most pessimistic observers. Millions were out of work and standing in soup lines as the Great Depression socked America. Banks failed. Businesses toppled. Shares in America's biggest companies were worth next to nothing. When people saw their life savings disappear, some of the most hopeless committed suicide, and tales of people jumping out of windows to their death were not uncommon. Like the 2008 economic meltdown, Ponzi schemes—only smaller—fueled the stock market's collapse in 1929. America immediately sank into a deep, long, heartbreaking depression. Hjalmar and Olga Nordstrand and Charles and Olga Swanson were sunk, too. No work, no income. The only comfort in their plight was the millions who joined them.

One of Grandpa Nordstrand's relatives suggested that he, once again, try farming in western Wisconsin. The struggling couple left Chicago, invested their savings, $8,000, and bought a ninety-acre farm and four-bedroom house without electricity five miles from Ellsworth, Wisconsin. Their adult sons, Art and Alvin, remained in Chicago.

Grandpa and Grandma Swanson and their two daughters decided to tough out the depression in the city, believing that it was the best place to find work.

A few years passed before Alvin Nordstrand convinced Helen Swanson to marry him on November 30, 1932. They had two witnesses: Dad's brother Arthur and his wife, Alice. Grandma Swanson cooked a delicious wedding dinner, and they took off that same night in a rickety Buick, bound for the Nordstrand farm. En route, the honeymoon couple ran out of gas, the engine broke down, and many hours passed before they finally pulled into the farmhouse driveway in tiny Ellsworth, Wisconsin, and lived there for the next thirty-four years.

AN OFFER AND A CHALLENGE

That farm was the best offer my newlywed parents had, though they knew nothing about farming. Grandpa and Grandma Nordstrand invited (some say commanded) Dad and Mom to live and work on the Nordstrand farm after their wedding. Living with their in-laws wasn't easy. Both Grandpa and Grandma had bouts of depression, a condition that went unrecognized and untreated in those days. Grandma called my mom "the dumbest thing" because she hadn't learned to cook, wash, or sew. At least Mom understood animals from her days on the Nebraska ranch. Dad had no farming skills, but his neighbor, the aforementioned Edgar, willingly coached him.

Friends and relatives in Chicago agreed on one thing: the young couple would never last in rural Ellsworth. But they underestimated my parents. They were stubbornly committed to making their life work on the farm. They would eventually buy the farm from Grandpa and Grandma Nordstrand, but in the meantime they adapted and persevered.

When Grandpa Nordstrand tore up the farmhouse kitchen to remodel it, Mom made do with a wood stove in the dining room. During that first winter, when Dad's brother Art and his wife lived on the farm with them, all three couples managed to share space in that blessedly large farmhouse. Dad cashed in his only insurance policy to purchase three cows for one hundred dollars. The investment led to a solid dairy business and a growing herd. With no farm machinery, Dad plowed his fields using a team of two unruly horses he painstakingly taught to plod in the same direction.

To help out, Mom raised about five hundred chicks each spring. On her own, and against the neighbor's advice, she drove a horse and buggy five miles to town to sell her hen's eggs. The trip took the whole day, but Mom unloaded her entire inventory for nine cents a dozen and returned home grinning with a big bag of groceries.

Mom and Dad bought a two-hundred-pound pig for seven dollars and had it butchered for three dollars so the family had roasts and chops all winter. With no refrigeration, Mom cooked and canned the meat. Produce from Mom's flourishing garden kept our pantry shelves stocked. The parade of summer visitors to our home always went back to Chicago with canned gifts from her cellar.

When the Rural Electrification Authority brought power to our farm in 1938, Mom and Dad no longer hand-pumped every drop of water for man and beast. Mom said good-bye to heating wash water on the wood stove and hand-washing clothes in a tub. Before long, they had an inside toilet, radiator heat, and household appliances. Decent farm machinery came next. Mom and Dad harvested more corn and raised more cattle than they ever dreamed they could. President Franklin D. Roosevelt made sure they earned fair income for their work.

The Nordstrand family made it through the Great Depression far better than many Americans. We always had shelter, warmth, and food on the table.

LOSSES AND GHOSTS

The family had their share of tragedies. When Mom and Dad welcomed their first child, Kenneth Duane, into the world on August 10, 1934, the farmhouse radiated with joy. Just three days later, when my Aunt Connie went to his crib, she found him dead. This was decades before we understood sudden infant death syndrome (SIDS). Kenneth was buried in the little Swedish Covenant Mission Church cemetery near our farm—the start of our family plot. Mom struggled with depression and loneliness for a long time after that. Others in my family did, too. Depression was a ghost for the Nordstrands, stretching back generations and making a home in my own psyche.

Only a year later on August 20, 1935, Mom and Dad greeted their second son, Dennis Leroy—the model kid with the achievement gene who would climb to one step shy of CEO at a large public company. Three years later on December 13—in a punishing snowstorm—I came along. I was the first Nordstrand kid delivered in a hospital, twelve miles west of Ellsworth in Red Wing, Minnesota. Thanks to the snow drifts, we were trapped in the hospital for a week. We limped home in our geriatric Buick. In retrospect, the circumstances of my birth were the first indication that Burton Lee Nordstrand was trouble.

RUNNING SCARED

There was nothing about farm work that I liked, but I had my chores morning and evening. I milked the cows, cleaned the barn, and drove our tractor in the fields by age ten. My brothers, Dennis and Ron, were much more willing. I recall Dad howling my nickname "Beeb" most mornings to get me up, have breakfast with him, and help with milking before school.

Ron still remembers seeing me catapulted from the back of the farm wagon when our dad forgot to secure the hitch pin. He also recalls a time when I chased him through a field during winter, trying to get him to take my cow-milking job. We scuffled and Ron was bloody. He retaliated by pricking me in the rearend with a pitchfork.

I remember having the first big shock of my young life when I helped Dad haul hay one afternoon and came upon my Grandpa Charles (Mom's father) dead on the ground. He was drawing water for our livestock, and his weak heart gave out.

Honestly, my dad ran scared most of the time. Maybe it started with being totally unprepared for the farm and having his parents "grade" his efforts. They visited every summer to survey the progress, and I imagine, Dad always fell short of their expectations.

Dad worried about everything—too little rain, too much rain, pests, seed costs, crop prices, harvest timing. He always worried about going broke, even though we had good crops, conveniences, and plenty of food. Farmers are, by nature, worriers, but Dad worried far more than most. His solution to utter failure on the farm was buying a motel in Iowa. He studied ads, and our family talked a lot about it. In reality, the motel was pure fantasy and escape for my father that he never pursued.

Though he was only in his thirties, Dad already had a bad back, leg pain, and other illnesses, real and imagined.—I remember seeing him crawl out to the barn when his back hurt too much to stand. His depression made the physical maladies worse. There were times he seemed so helpless, so sad. In later years, he threatened suicide. His own father, Hjalmar, actually went through with it years before.

I believe Dad was an alcoholic who only allowed himself

occasional binges—the most predictable before and after fall threshing, when our neighborhood collectively harvested our grain. All the men gathered at a pre-threshing meeting to plan the assault on our fields. Beer flowed freely, thanks to local tavern owners who delivered free cases. The same routine occurred at the "settle-up" meeting after threshing. Each time, Dad drank beer until he nearly passed out. And sometimes did. The addict in Dad showed up in other compulsive behaviors. He smoked four packs a day. If we had a box of chocolates, he ate the whole box. If he had chewing gum, he tore through a package. I learned later to get on his right side with offers of sweets (the budding con artist in me knew how to get my way). Though Dad was a compulsive overeater, he worked so hard, he stayed trim.

Mom's life was absorbed by Dad's fears and physical ailments. She propped him up and paid little attention to her children, assuming, I suppose, that we were resourceful and resilient. Mom was almost invisible to us; but, in reality, she was the "pit bull" in our family, wielding her influence in the background. The strong, tenacious one. The survivor.

Mom's social life revolved around the telephone party line, the church, Ladies Aid Society, and frequent summer visits from friends and family escaping the Chicago heat. She planned for our many guests with the precision of a star quarterback executing the best calls. Long after Dad died, Mom was the glue that held our family together. She kept track of all the new additions to our family, followed our lives and missteps without judgment, staged our family gatherings, and never lost touch of anyone. She was a quiet marvel.

People often told me how lucky I was to have such wonderful parents and a comfortable home. Hearing that, I silently wondered, *Then why do we live in so much fear? Why do I feel so bad most of the time?*

I didn't share this with my siblings. Instead, I hid my feelings with extravagant demonstrations of optimism and enthusiasm. And, in later years—as if to rebel against the gnawing fear—I took financial risks. Fear was a permanent feature in my life for decades.

IF SOME IS GOOD, MORE IS BETTER

Depression, addiction, pursuing the sugar "high"—all of these qualities that stalked my father, stalked me, too. I discovered the mood-altering power of sugar and carbs when my appendix burst at age nine. We drove on slippery roads in December to the closest hospital, in Red Wing, Minnesota. The last thing I remember before the anesthesia kicked in was my doctor singing, "You'll be home for Christmas." My December 13th birthday was coming up, and we expected a big gang of family and neighbors for Christmas dinner. Homemade ice cream was a highlight, and I was allowed to eat all I wanted that year. That's when I discovered the buzz, the euphoria, the contentment of a sugar high. Consuming sugar was the easiest way to escape pain, and I used sugar to alter my mood from then on. I also discovered that carbs, especially bread and chips, offered the same high because carbs converted to sugar in my body.

Decades passed before the facts about sugar became clear. By 2009, America's consumption of high-fructose corn syrup had increased by forty times, with Americans eating three hundred more calories of sugar a day. Researchers learned that too much sugar not only adds calories, raising the risk of obesity, it also speeds up aging, contributes to Type 2 diabetes, raises our blood fats (triglycerides) to dangerous levels, and contributes to cancer. We have also learned that some people are "sugar sensitive." They are born with low levels of two important brain chemicals: serotonin and dopamine. People who are sugar sensitive are more prone to depression, aggression, poor attention, impulse control, addiction, low self-esteem, and anger. They usually have volatile blood sugar levels, too; and that's associated with moodiness, fatigue, and diabetes. Like an addict looking for a fix, sugar-sensitive people seek out foods that make them feel better, no matter how short-lived that relief might be. If that addiction starts early in life, there's a higher risk of drug and alcohol addiction in adulthood. Was I sugar sensitive as a kid? Absolutely.

Feeding my embryonic sugar habit was easy. Edgar, Vernon, and Les obliged with treats at the bar almost every day. And when fall came, threshing was a food blowout.

The women baked their best pies and cakes and served up huge noon-time dinners during the threshing season, which lasted as long as three weeks. This was the biggest social event of the year, and the men usually got fresh haircuts and new bib overalls in preparation. Even as children, we had jobs to do as our team of neighbors moved from farm to farm, loading bundles of oats, putting them through the threshing machine to separate the oats from the straw, and delivering the final loads to the granary. I remember driving a farm wagon as the men pitched oat bundles into the wagon. They put me in the top of the granary to level off the new piles of finished oats, and my goal was not to get buried in the process. By the noon meal, I was ravenous, and at the end of the day, I swigged quarts of sugar-laden pop while the men consumed cases of beer.

Our home was always the gathering place for neighborhood celebrations, and Sunday dinner attracted neighbors, teachers, and our minister. Mom served up roasted chicken, baked beans, scalloped potatoes, rice pudding, and homemade bread, her specialty. The food was limitless, and I had no limits.

I looked forward to the county fairs because I could binge on sweets, pop, and fried foods. I was pretty much on my own by age ten. I usually entered a calf as a 4-H project, but I never actually raised it. I borrowed the calf from my neighbors, Everett and Marion; and Edgar, my bachelor buddy, helped me make the calf presentable. Edgar usually drove me to the fair, about five miles from home. I turned a three-day event into four days with no adult supervision. I slept in the barn with my calf and hung out with the carnies on the midway, eating everything I wanted. That was my first exposure to professional con men, and I discovered I could con the carnies just as well as they conned me. I was charming, conniving, and manipulative; and I spent a lifetime refining those skills learned at the country fair.

The Minnesota State Fair in St. Paul was a family event—the only vacation my parents ever took. We'd find someone to take the farm chores for one day, we'd leave at six A.M. and travel sixty miles for a long day of livestock shows, midway rides, freak shows, and games of chance. Again, I ate and drank everything I wanted, and my parents didn't seem to notice.

The county and state fairs were like threshing day in the fall—only on steroids. Years later, I had to laugh when I learned that Ellsworth, the home of Burton Nordstrand, compulsive overeater, had also become the "cheese curd capital" of Wisconsin.

When I needed money to buy candy bars and pop, I went through my mom's handbag, Dad's wallet, or the collection plate at church. I landed odd jobs to earn pocket money, too. I usually ate in private, which is what most addicts do. Look at my childhood photos, and you'll see an overweight kid. I knew there was something wrong with what I was doing and how I did it. It showed on my chubby face and fed a deep insecurity in me. The cycle had begun: the worse I felt, the more I ate. The more I ate, the worse I felt.

MONEY TALKS

That's why I think it was easy for my parents to loosen the reins. Beginning at about age ten, I spent three summers in Springfield, Missouri, with Grandpa and Grandma Nordstrand and Dad's brother Arthur and his wife, Alice. Grandpa and Art were both contractors, and they worked on large projects together. Over those years, the two couples lived next door to each other.

The experience was positive for me because I learned to earn and handle money. I saw a world I never knew existed—what life was like in the city. I also discovered how much sadness pervaded the lives of my grandparents.

Though some considered her a tyrant, Grandma Nordstrand was kind to me. She got me a bicycle and made my lunch every day. I rode to Salzan's fruit stand to work. I sold fruit all day, then biked home to carefully count the day's tips with Grandma. She taught me about finances and saving. I learned to play tennis on a neighbor's court and landed a job as a caddy at an exclusive country club. My co-workers and friends were black; the people I knew in Ellsworth were lily-white. I discovered what the "good life" looked like and noticed how people treated each other. I learned some manners, and I saw the power of money in action.

Grandpa Nordstrand was retired by that time. He often told stories of his days as a superintendent on big construction jobs in Chicago during the gangland days of Al Capone. Grandpa was tough, hardworking and successful. He and my Uncle Art, a successful builder and contractor, were my first positive role models in business. I recall dropping off to sleep in my bed at home on the farm, years later, hearing the hog feeder clank shut when our herd finished eating. That sound gave me an idea: I wanted to figure out how I could make money while I slept! Now *that* would be success.

But Grandpa had his dark side, too. I remember overhearing my grandparents talk about their lives. There was so much sadness and pain in what they said; it shocked me. Grandpa kept saying, "I've never done anything right for you ... or for anybody...."

That stayed with me. Grandpa was two people: the strong, successful public man and the sad, brooding private man. That's where I learned I could put on a good front, even when I was crumbling inside.

SUGAR MADE ME HIGH, THEN IT TOOK AWAY THE SKY

I knew I had to buck up when I turned nine and six of us were bused in a station wagon to Ellsworth Grade School, some five miles from home. Good-bye to the one-room schoolhouse and kids who looked just like me. Now, I was the farm kid with bib overalls who smelled faintly of cow manure. The town kids dressed differently, and I was teased. Even when Mom bought me new clothes, my insecurities didn't lift. I was the odd kid, less-than, found wanting. That confirmed what I always believed: I was different and I would never fit in.

That was the same year my appendix burst and I ate ice cream until I got sick.

Sick or not, sugar took me away from the things that hurt, especially how I felt about myself. All through school, I tried to be the class clown but that backfired. I just looked stupid most of the time. Though I had a good brain, studying was tough for me. Heavy sugar doses kept me distracted, and I couldn't concentrate. My mind was busy. It wandered. I lived in my own little world and kept packing on the pounds. Though I had trouble studying, the sugar high was my survival tool, giving me the gumption to pursue money-making schemes.

I was about thirteen when my parents took me to the doctor and I got my first prescription for diet pills, the start of a speed addiction that later had me searching for backroom docs with few scruples. Even as a young teenager, I learned to work the black-market prescription meds scene. Not only did they help me lose weight, the pills gave me another fast way to get high. I was addicted.

But there was more to feed my plummeting self-esteem than weight alone. Dad and I visited the doctor again when I was four-teen—this time to examine my male organs. I remember his asking the doctor in a hushed voice he thought I couldn't hear, "Is he going to be a man?"

The doctor answered "yes," but the question was more painful than the answer was reassuring. Once a week, I left school early on Friday afternoon to get my shot. Drawing attention to myself by leaving school made me feel even worse. When I asked, my mother could never explain what the shot was for, but I imagine it was a growth hormone. Leaving school early was embarrassing. It only confirmed how different I was. Inside, I had stinging self-doubt. *Would I grow up like Edgar, my neighbor, after all? How could anyone really like me if I was fat? I'll never have a girlfriend.* I was an outcast. *I might as well eat.*

Many years later, I found the right words to describe how I felt: I had a hole in my soul.

BEING FONZIE

By the time I hit high school in 1952, I was a budding juvenile delinquent stealing money from stores for food and alcohol; shoplifting cigarettes; siphoning gas for my friend's car; hanging out at local bars with Edgar, Vernon, and Les; and planning fairly innocent capers by future standards with other troublemakers from my school. I even involved Ron in an aborted plan to "pave" Main Street with fresh manure. My friends were people who helped me pull off my schemes and feed my habits. Skipping class, I barely averaged a D on report cards, which I conveniently lost before my parents saw them. Next to my senior picture in my yearbook was a statement summarizing my high school career: "Just dropped into class to see what's goin' on." My teacher echoed what I already believed about myself: "Burton," she advised, with hurtful candor, "you'll never get to first base."

I proudly wore the Fonzie uniform: slick, black hair combed into a ducktail, motorcycle boots, Marlboros folded into my tee-shirt sleeve, tight jeans. I even had a motor bike that my dad helped me buy. I liked to think that girls stayed away because they thought I was dangerous. I certainly didn't appeal to those perfect girls in confirmation class. I wouldn't have known what to do with them if they showed interest anyway. I didn't know how to act around girls, so I didn't experiment with sex.

When the county sheriff visited Mom and told her he was "concerned about Burt," I had to clean up my act. A little.

What I needed was money to buy sugar, alcohol, cigarettes, and black market diet pills.

Even as a kid, I had a knack for making money. During World War II when I was six or seven, I had picked milk weed pods with my brother Dennis. We made ten cents on a batch of pods, and the government used the silk to make parachutes. As a teenager, I worked deals with kids who were as sneaky as I was. One friend stole clothes from his father's department store and sold them to me for ten percent of the ticket price. I re-sold the goods. I sold year-old Christmas Seals as a charity fundraiser and pocketed the income. I hawked *Agriculture* magazine and became their top salesman. A subscription was a dollar a year, and I made ninety cents. Rather than sell customers on just one year, though, I'd sell five-year subscriptions that came with a prize. The backseat of my car was piled high with pliers, hammers, pots, and stepladders that I bought for next to nothing from the magazine company. The free gift for five-year subscriptions almost always worked.

I was never without money in my pocket and a cool car. Why? I was becoming an accomplished con artist. The skill goes back to when I was nine years old and discovered that I had to have sugar. I was a lovable con who manipulated my family, friends, and strangers. Conning got me sugar, then it got me much more. Conning worked in business, and it worked in many other aspects of life.

TWO

LEARNING TO LIVE LARGE

SEEDS OF DOUBT

My lungs ache. I'm inhaling dust. Sweat stings my eyes. This is hell on Earth, and it's nearly that hot. The sarge at Camp McCoy has it in for me.

We're up before dawn at Army Reserve summer camp—two weeks of "yes sir, no sir (up yours, sir)," and it feels like six months. The calisthenics at dawn nearly kill me, even though I'm accustomed to farm work. Aerobic exercise for a 220-pound, six-foot tall, undisciplined kid of seventeen is lethal.

Even worse, I'm not growing a beard yet and the sarge has noticed. While I struggle with a set of rapid-fire push-ups, he scans my pale, slack body and spits out a cruel nickname: "Seedless." He finds plenty of reason to shout it out when I can't keep pace. I'm secretly worrying that I'll turn out like my poor neighbor, Edgar. Not man enough.

I'm assigned to the 373rd Panel Bridge Company, and we're building temporary bridges. I've never seen so much discipline in my life. When we're on bivouac duty, we sleep in tents in the field, exercise until our lungs nearly burst, and simulate combat by crawling under barbed wire and leaping over fences while our "enemies" use live ammunition. It's terrifying. Painful. Embarrassing.

And I'm a target—not just for my sarge or our made-up enemy. I never told anyone this: one night on bivouac, a guy I knew crawled into my tent and started fondling me. I responded to his advances for a few seconds in my sleep. Then I snapped awake and slugged him. What is it about me? Maybe I'm sending out the wrong vibes. Maybe I *am* seedless. I felt immense shame for years, until I realized this wasn't an uncommon occurrence for young guys.

My high school buddies joined the Army Reserves on a lark, and I just went along. Maybe I liked the uniform. I was still in high school, and I sure didn't fit in there. I thought the Reserves would be different—a fraternity of tough guys where I *did* fit in.

YOU'RE IN THE ARMY, NOW

Whatever my reasons were, it was a good time to be in uniform. I committed to serve for seven years. The Korean War ended in 1953, and American boys were back home after defending the freedom of democratic South Korea from the invasion of communist-led North Korea. There were no wars to fight, and we had a retired supreme commander in the White House, Dwight D. Eisenhower.

Everybody liked "Ike," our World War II hero/president. When I joined the Army Reserve in 1955, Ike was finishing his first term. When I enlisted in 1956, Ike was campaigning for his second. Our whole neighborhood drove to Red Wing to see him deliver a stump speech from the back of his campaign train. Democrats even liked him.

Ellsworth High School was glad to see me go. I had scraped by with poor grades and barely graduated. Though I signed up for football, basketball, and baseball, I rarely played. I was undisciplined, and the coach couldn't count on me. I lied to my parents about being chosen class secretary when no one even nominated me. I was desperate for their approval.

That pretty girl in the white, embroidered collar, with the knockout smile would never get any closer than appearing beside me on page eighteen in the Ellsworth yearbook. She was a "Future Homemaker of America," an officer, and a smart girl in Library Club. I was all show, no go.

At least I had the gumption to go to Camp Leonard Wood in Springfield, Missouri, for six months of Army Reserve basic training with my five buddies. If Camp McCoy in Wisconsin was blazing hot in the summers, our basic training camp in Missouri was bone-chilling cold from October through March 1957. We slept in tents, and I never got warm. When you scan the faces of the soldiers, I'm the one with the chunkiest cheeks. There are also a lot of non-white faces. This was my first exposure to an integrated society aside from my summer visits to my grandparents in Springfield—a long way from harmonious, homogeneous Ellsworth.

SURVIVAL SKILLS

I earned a sharp-shooting medal with my M1 rifle. That finally gave me reason to be proud. I became a certified "automotive maintenance helper" following basic training, so I had a job. My teen bravado didn't pass muster in the Army. I learned survival by shutting up and swallowing my fear. I did it when I got an emergency call, and the soldier who relayed the message said both my parents were killed in a car accident. The truth was that my Grandpa Nordstrand died. He committed suicide in his closed garage with his car running.

I sucked up my fear again when a fellow soldier demanded money and threatened me with a switchblade to my throat in an empty stairwell. I gave him my cash and never spoke of it again. I instinctively understood power and powerlessness ... and I drew the short straw.

With time, I was determined to build my own power base, and it was not going to happen in the Army garage where I worked. That's why I applied to be "second cook" in the mess hall, even though I didn't know how to cook. Cooks had power. No one knew your rank, because cooks wore white, not uniforms. We supervised enlisted men who were assigned KP duty. We had access to the kitchen stores, and I could snack all I wanted. If the company sergeant wanted an extra five pounds of coffee, I could make it happen (in exchange for a favor). The first cook and I traded food for favors, including three-day passes and clothing controlled by the supply sergeant. I refined my con game by making deals and testing the Army's limits to see how much I could get away with. That's how I protected my supply of diet pills, too. Even during my months at Fort Leonard Wood, I had those contraband pills to counteract my food and sugar binges.

On leave, alcohol and cigarettes had only passing appeal, though I added them to my pack of addictions soon enough. When I drank and smoked, I wanted to look cool and worldly around women. I didn't have a single date in the service, and I only *wondered* about sex. All I knew about sex was what I learned from the alcoholic bachelor farmers of Ellsworth.

LIFE'S A GAMBLE

Arriving home from Fort Leonard Wood, I had a blinding flash of the obvious—if I was going to support my addiction to food and diet pills, I had to either steal money or earn it. My self-worth was tied to having money; that's how I kept score. I had utter confidence in my money-making ability.

I took odds jobs. I sold tire repair kits to gas stations and did it with a convincing show. If I had nothing else, I always managed to own an impressive car. I drove that polished badge of success into a station and invited the owner outside saying, "I want to show you something." Before he could answer, I jammed an ice pick into my tire. *Now what?* the guy wondered. I pulled out my revolutionary product: a tubeless tire repair kit. The device looked like an ice pick with an "eye" on one end. I strung an eight-inch piece of nylon material through the eye and pushed it through the tire hole. After turning the "pick" a few times, I pulled the nylon out a bit and cut the exposed end with a razor blade to be flush with the tire surface. The nylon adhered to the inside of the tire and fixed the leak.

The demo never failed, and I always sold kits.

In another entrepreneurial venture, I bought a thousand ballpoint pens for ten cents each when they were new on the market. I quickly sold each one for a buck.

I sanded the insides of caves in Diamond Bluff, Wisconsin, for a guy who unsuccessfully planned to paint the caves with latex and store bins of natural gas there. I sorted letters at the post office during the Christmas holidays.

In my worst job, I spent the whole day removing cooked hams from a cooker the size of a small garage and putting them on a conveyor belt at the Armour and Company packing plant in South St. Paul. During my lunch break, I walked though the hog butchering department to the company cafeteria, and before I made it halfway, the odor was so bad that I threw up. On the way back with a full stomach, I'd lose my lunch again. The reaction was so common; Armor put a "barf barrel" at the door.

Finally, I got a job at American Hoist & Derrick Company in St. Paul where my brother Dennis was climbing the corporate ladder. I started out as a chipper grinder—the guy who chipped the excess off a welded part and ground it smooth in the manufacturing process. Next, I became a forklift driver and, finally, a clerk in the shipping department where I had access to all of AmHoist's five hundred employees and plant locations. I made my rounds with deliveries and started my own numbers racket on the side, selling pull tabs, ballpoint pens, and taking bets on football and basketball games. I walked around with my deliveries and a clipboard, keeping track of my little side businesses. Over time, I hooked up with another bookie and took more and larger bets. The money was good, but I had my first cliffhanger when I lost a couple thousand bucks (the equivalent of six months' salary) and I couldn't cover it. I got a loan to pay back the bookie, but the incident scared me. I swore off gambling. Briefly.

I had become obsessed with making a lot of money. Gambling was the ticket, but money wasn't the only prize. The action attracted me—the thrill of the deal, the risk of the bet, the adrenaline rush of the play. It was a new way to get high.

HELL ON WHEELS

When I discovered irresponsible sex, I found another way to feel a rush. After years of standing on the sidelines, at age twenty I met Pat Murphy in 1958. In those days, I still lived at home and the Wisconsin taverns were my refuge for friendship and entertainment. All of it was so familiar from the countless afternoons I hung out with Edgar or Vernon at the Ellsworth bars.

Now my hangouts were farther from home. The setting was classic: dim light; creaky, wood floors; garish, neon beer signs over the bar; smoke mixed with sweat and hops; Johnny Cash on the jukebox; and a live country western band on weekends. Pat was a cute, dark-haired secretary from a strong, Catholic family. Great figure. Willing to endure my beginner's sex—a thirty-second climax in the backseat of my car. I was a total amateur, but even so, Pat grew to care.

That amazed me. I never really felt attractive. I was embarrassed and self-conscious, so I started a "controlled eating" plan and managed to look pretty good. I tried to act cool, and the alcohol helped. By that time, I had all my addictions firing: sugar, cigarettes, booze, caffeine, prescription drugs, sex, gambling, making money. When they did, I always felt better about myself. I was funny and I charmed people.

I could sell Burt, just like I hawked magazines, Christmas seals, and tire repair kits. Feeling more confident, I made a decision to play it straight and not make my money as a con artist, though even my "straight days" had shades of gray.

Pat's attention thrilled me, but I was skeptical, too. In my deep insecurity, I reasoned that anyone who liked *me* must not be too good herself. *Maybe,* I secretly thought, *we were both damaged goods?*

Through the summer, our backseat experiments in sex multiplied and the inevitable happened. Pat was pregnant.

In my young, insecure brain, the only answer was marriage. I wasn't one of those cut-and-run guys. If Pat liked me that much, I better marry her. I might not find anyone else. The Protestant-Catholic divide meant little to us, and neither Pat nor I planned to convert. We planned to go to the courthouse. My parents were supportive and even offered to buy furniture for the little one-bedroom apartment in Prescott, Wisconsin, that we picked as our first home.

We were happy about our plans until Pat called me after work. "My parents want us to meet at the church," she said. That evening, I walked into the priest's study at Big River Catholic Church. Pat and her parents sat beside Father Antoine, positioned behind his ornate desk that seemed three feet off the ground. I felt small, insignificant, powerless.

Pat's parents told us we'd go to hell if we married outside the Catholic Church, and the priest offered his most harrowing definition of hell: "Let me tell you how long hell is, my children. If you take a pebble of sand off the beach every million years, you would never clear the beach. Hell is eternity."

Pat's tearful mother recalled her daughter's childhood when she developed rheumatic fever. "I prayed to God," she whispered to Pat, loud enough so I could hear, "if you let her live, I'll say the rosary every day for my whole life." She stared coldly at Pat, delivering the gut punch, "Now I wish I had just let you die."

My memory of what happened next is impossible to reconstruct. Pat and I were outnumbered. Pat's parents and the priest had God on their side and the double whammy of religious and parental authority. I remember feeling ashamed and guilty. My mother stepped into my room to comfort me—one of the rare times in my life. We never discussed the showdown at the church or the aborted marriage, though my parents somehow knew the details.

The next day, Pat left town, six months pregnant. I never saw her again, and no one told me where the home for unwed mothers was located. Pat married six months after delivering her baby. Her new husband adopted my son and never told him he had a different father until he needed a passport at age twenty-one. My grown son called me, and we got acquainted for the first time. Like me, Tim never attended college, but he was a natural in business and a born entrepreneur. He and I talk from time to time, and we stay connected, but I regret that I was unable to know him during his childhood.

I'M YOUR MAN

I was a failure in my first, and still only, relationship with a woman; but I knew how to make money. I always had cash in my pocket, and by 1960, I was driving the hottest car around, a Buick Wildcat.

I didn't have any role models in business, except my Uncle Art, the contractor, and Grandpa Nordstrand, the tough Swedish carpenter. Even so, I decided that if I was going to *be somebody*, the fuel that fired my success would be business. What did I need with an education or MBA? I had the street smarts, confidence, and willingness to do what I had to do.

That's what John P. O'Malley saw in me one night in an Ellsworth tavern. I was twenty-four, recently laid off at American Hoist and Derrick, and hanging out playing cards with my bachelor farmer buddies. In walked this bigger-than-life Irishman with a grin and a swagger. He was about ten years older, six feet tall, and pushing 250 pounds, and I couldn't take my eyes off him. I had to find out who he was.

In those days, gas was cheap and plentiful, selling for twelve to fifteen cents a gallon, without the tax. The country was flying high. John F. Kennedy was on his way to winning the presidency and introducing Americans to his version of Camelot. The country had eighty-five million TV sets, and the American Heart Association issued its first report declaring that middle-aged men who were heavy smokers cut their lives short.

John O'Malley represented Bell Northern Oil Company. He traveled Wisconsin, his home state, looking for places to buy land and build cut-rate gas stations to fuel America's love affair with cars. He described these operations as "a shade tree with an umbrella and a couple pumps out front selling regular and ethyl." Simple, straightforward. Easy to build. No more than a $15,000 to $20,000 investment per station. After that, the profit was steady.

Wisconsin could have all the gas it wanted because Bell Northern shipped gas from its refinery in Texas through the Great Lakes Pipeline to the Midwest. John sold gas for Bell, just like his dad before him. He fascinated me because he knew a little about everything. He talked about railroads and engineering. He described every step of the refining process and made it sound like a riveting novel. He seemed to know every word in the dictionary. He even recited some poetry. John was a study in contrasts: in the tavern, he wore a checkered, lumberjack shirt, but he looked just as comfortable in a three-piece tailored suit at oilman conventions. He had the intellect to discuss literature and the life experience to trade low-life tales with the boys. John P. O'Malley was success personified: ambitious, big thinking, and charming.

While we talked, John told me he'd picked out property for a gas station on the main highway outside Ellsworth. All he needed was a good manager. Before John took his next breath, I leaped at the chance:

"I'll help you build the station and run it. I'm your man."

John didn't give me an answer that day, but he called the next and told me I had the job. Though I had no experience, it didn't seem to bother him. O'Malley saw himself in me—and how right he was.

INITIATIVE AND INGENUITY

We hired a local carpenter to build the ten-by-twenty-foot gas station. John and I found another helper, and we built the storage tanks, poured the concrete island, and installed four gas pumps. The driveway was gravel with not enough subsoil. When it rained, customers' cars sometimes got stuck.

Bell Northern let me name the station "Burt's Gas for Less," and I had a sign made. Coke gave me a free road sign if I advertised their product. Because other stations carried brand names like Phillips or Standard, I attracted customers to my no-name gas by dropping the price a couple cents per gallon. I made a commission on each sale, and the sales started to climb.

I invented another way to set myself apart from the competition. In those days, a station pumped gas and did mechanical work. In addition, I added a little convenience. I borrowed one hundred dollars from my dad to buy motor oil, candy bars, soda, gum, cigarettes. My customers loved it, and the profit on those sales was all my own.

Through the years, my dad supported my business ideas, even though some seemed hare brained. That gave me confidence, but Dad's support was sporadic and confusing. Years later as my own company grew dramatically, Dad never acknowledged my success. I wanted to please him, but I never felt I did.

My station made the newspaper when I invited friends and the local editor to witness Ada Gerlitz, a gal with shapely legs, daintily place her foot into the wet cement for posterity—ala Grauman's Chinese Restaurant in Hollywood. Later, I got free publicity again when I handed out free, miniature American flags to every customer on the Fourth of July.

By talking up my business at local taverns, I convinced local farmers to take home delivery on gas for their tractors and fuel oil to heat their homes. I found an old truck that Bell paid for, painted it bright orange with a big blue "Bell" on the side, and started selling gas and oil in bulk. When I made two or three cents a gallon on five hundred gallons in home deliveries, my profits were impressive. I opened an account at the Bank of Ellsworth and qualified for a line of credit to cover daily expenses. Remarkably, "the Fonz" was becoming a respected businessman.

My salesmanship and charm went into high gear. I had no doubts about my ability and my confidence attracted people. Friends from the old days became regular customers, and they told others. I promoted my station on regular trips to the taverns where I bought rounds for the boys. O'Malley, my mentor and cheerleader, loved it. When he came to Ellsworth, we had lavish dinners with unlimited drinks and we spun visions of growth and prosperity. We charmed each other and the "courtship" was as intoxicating as any seduction I'd ever imagined with a woman. O'Malley believed in me. He ran about a dozen gas stations in Wisconsin, and my little operation was one of the best. He wanted to make me more successful because, when I looked good, he looked good.

We had the same appetites: plentiful and virtually insatiable.

LIVING LARGE

John O'Malley was my first mentor and a huge life force. I admired his intelligence and savviness. We enjoyed each other immensely and became best friends. John took me to petroleum conventions in Wisconsin, Minnesota, and Illinois, where people in the business promoted their products and made their deals. They did it in hospitality rooms loaded with more exotic food and drink than I had ever seen. It was better than any state fair I remembered from childhood.

The conventions were like cocaine for me. There I was, "the Fonz," spiffed up in a three-piece suit, mixing with oilmen, drinking and noshing with my heavy-drinking pal, John O'Malley. Naturally we had access to women—prostitutes lingering in the hotel hallways and lounges. I was no better at sex, but the alcohol helped. John was a family man, but he kept his party life separate. This was my first exposure to "boxes." I saw the advantages of keeping one aspect of my life separate from another. No overlap. No regrets. But these types of "boxes" are an illusion. People around us always see more than we realize.

Before long, John asked me to go on the road with him and become his assistant. He wanted me to learn the big picture and start supervising multiple stations. John moved his office from his home in Madison, Wisconsin, to LaCrosse and left the road to me. I moved to LaCrosse and lived with his family for a while.

Now, I had a company car, an unlimited expense account, and power. I supervised fifteen stations, and fifteen managers reported to me. During those years, we hired Larry Hopkins, a bookkeeper who worked with me from then on.

I scouted new locations, negotiated offers on land, and supervised construction of more gas stations. I ate whatever I wanted: chips, peanuts, doughnuts, candy bars, sodas. The high from sugar and carbs gave me the energy to move fast and think faster.

I bought a Bell gas station in Whitehall, Wisconsin, and leased it back to the company. That way, I generated more income for myself. I was learning the law of leveraging, and I did it more. If I found an ideal location for another station, I offered to buy it and then I leased it back to Bell. I figured I could pay off each investment in five years. I took advantage of my friendship with John to push for more opportunities and income.

There was a lot of partying in the off hours with O'Malley, schmoozing in the taverns, and sometimes hooking up with women (though none led to a real relationship). I liked the high that went with drinking, sex, and being a big-shot-in-training.

When John and I went to the Twin Cities, we enjoyed only the best—butter knife steaks at Murray's and steak tartar and bourbon at Charlie's, where the Minneapolis big shots did deals.

As my bank account grew and my business life became more successful, I started treating my parents with gifts. I hoped they would see me differently than the young juvenile delinquent who worried them in high school. I wanted to show them I had more going for me. I bought my parents their first color TV set and installed a furnace in their farmhouse. They didn't really need my help, but I felt it was an unspoken expectation. I never forgot how my dad worried about money; I think he hoped I would take care of him and Mom in their later years.

ROLL THE DICE

I was tireless in business; I was fueled by sugar, alcohol, caffeine, diet pills, gambling, and loads of ambition. O'Malley had taught me well, and by 1963, I wanted more. It was an implausible year. Our whole world turned upside down when Lee Harvey Oswald gunned down President Kennedy. Everything seemed up in the air. Why not roll the dice on my career, too?

I heard about a new job at Oskey Brothers Petroleum Company, a St. Paul–based company owned by Northwestern Refining. They supplied independent-station operators with their own brand of gasoline called North Star. They also sold wholesale gas to anyone who wanted it. Oskey wanted a man to start a new division focused on creating company-owned and operated gas stations in the Twin Cities.

I had all the skills for that job and mountains of confidence. O'Malley reluctantly said good-bye to our working relationship, believing Oskey offered me more. This was a bigger chance to be an entrepreneur using other people's money and resources to build a business. I set up my new division in a little office suite at the back of a warehouse in St. Paul, hired my own secretary, and met two men who became mentors and close friends: Jim Emison, Oskey's sales manager, and Len Jaskowiak, the company's credit manager. They were each a decade older than I, experienced, worldly, and prodigious drinkers like me.

O'Malley remained with Bell Northern until that company began to deteriorate. As my business was growing, he worked for me briefly, but my shift from protégé to his boss rankled him. It made working together impossible. O'Malley hit his career peak in his thirties and never ascended further. I think alcohol contributed to it. He died in

2007, after complications from, among other things, an attack in his Texas trailer house by a stranger armed with a two-by-four.

The first two gas stations I acquired for Oskey Brothers were located at 28th and Cedar in Minneapolis and 4040 Marshall in Northeast Minneapolis. My job was to operate them profitably and find other locations to build. Next came our Ellsworth store where Burt, the hometown boy, was a big hit. I bought land and built the new station/convenience store and demonstrated my flair for promotion with a two-day grand opening. I hosted TV personality, Clancy the Cop, and gave away prizes, including bikes, Tonka toys, trading stamps for free gas, and a set of four highball glasses for each driver who came to my station. At the Ellsworth station, we experimented with selling household and sporting goods and lawn and garden tools, in the same way that two brand-new ventures, Holiday and SuperAmerica, did. Of course, we also carried our signature "convenience foods"—lots of snacks, sodas, and cigarettes.

GOING IT ALONE

After a couple years with Oskey, my entrepreneurial instincts kicked in again. Oskey's gas stations were just a small part of the company's total revenue, but they represented a big chance for me. Rather than expand that new division, I convinced Verne Oskey to lease the stations to me and let me run them independently. I would still be a North Star dealer, and I'd add more stores. This idea added up to fewer headaches for Oskey and more, clear profit.

Sold. The idea felt good. Though I never called myself an entrepreneur in those days, I had all the characteristics. I was a self-starter, full of optimism and ambition. I equated risk with opportunity, *not* the chance of failure. I often envisioned possibilities where they didn't exist. I wasn't discouraged by naysayers. Other people's rules and bureaucracies only made me antsy. I'd sooner defy authority than conform. (Some of the most successful entrepreneurs started out just like me: poor in school, loners, people who felt they never fit in, people with something to prove—the same characteristics often shared by addicts.)

I lived on Lake Harriet at the time with my young wife, Sharon, and I set up my office in my home. In June 1967, I opened a new North Star station in Shakopee and made it memorable. I hired two good-looking women wearing fishnet stockings, skimpy costumes, and rabbit ears like Hugh Hefner's famous *Playboy* Bunnies. They became my "bumper bunnies" for the grand opening and they actually pumped gas, causing quite a stir in that little suburban town just south of the Twin Cities.

At my inner city Minneapolis station, business was touch and go. America was in turmoil. Thousands of people marched in Washington against U.S. involvement in the Vietnam War. More protests erupted in New York and San Francisco. At the same time, Martin Luther King Jr. was leading rallies to promote civil rights for blacks in America. Race riots erupted during the sweltering summer in Cleveland, Newark, and Detroit. Even North and South Minneapolis saw some marching, looting, and burning. My gas station was not far from the action, and I had some customers who looked pretty menacing. I was the target of threats, too. But nothing stopped me. Photos from that era show me washing car windows and grinning. Serve the customer with a smile. Keep 'em coming back.

IRWIN, THE BAG MAN

In 1969, I took a phone call from Irwin Jacobs—a call that sent me spinning into the entrepreneurial stratosphere. This was long before Irwin parlayed his business savvy into high-visibility ventures, acquisitions, and hostile takeovers. When his portfolio included Lund boats, Polaris snowmobiles, and partnerships with Carl Pohlad, the big financier and Twins baseball team owner, Irwin was an undisputed big player. But for now, he was a hungry, young entrepreneur in his late twenties, just like me. Irwin and I were a lot alike. No education beyond high school. Street smart gamblers. Driven.

Irwin was a shining star in the Twin Cities' tight-knit Jewish community. He and his father ran Northwestern Bag Company, a family business that bought trainloads of gunny sacks and sold them to towns for flood relief. People filled those bags with sand and stacked them up to hold back the rising flood waters. Irwin and his father used their business smarts to buy and salvage all kinds of used goods; they had an uncanny ability to make money.

Irwin was calling me with an idea. He, his brother-in-law, and a few other investors had just taken their Sonny's Discount Stores public. In those days, deals were flowing like the Mighty Mississippi and some people took companies public that had no business doing so. The local over-the-counter (OTC) stock market was hot; rumors fueled public offerings to raise operating capital for everything from bakeries to semiconductors. Minneapolis was a center for investment in "glamour" stocks of the day—companies like Xerox, Texas Instruments, and Medtronic. People lined up over their lunch hour at fly-by-night investment firms waiting to buy stocks of all kinds. Some people used their grocery money on highly speculative ventures. They might as well have tossed dice. "Dollar" stocks opened at three to four dollars when trading started and multiplied up to twenty times in a day. Some people made a lot of money, but more people got hurt.

Irwin and his partners had raised $300,000 in their public offering for Sonny's Discount Stores. They had two locations. Dayton Hudson Company had introduced its new discount concept, Target Stores, six years earlier in Minnesota, and Irwin was convinced the business model was sound. He called me because he wanted to offer gas station services at Sonny's store locations. He'd seen me successfully combine gas and goods already. SuperAmerica (owned by Northwestern Refining) and Holiday (owned by the Minnesota Erickson family) were just taking off, too. Customers wanted convenience *and* bargains; and Minnesota's entrepreneurs were up to the challenge.

Irwin offered to merge with my company, Norco Oil, build more gas stations, and stock them with discount merchandise. He paid me about $75,000 in cash and the rest in stock. I became vice president, reporting to the president. This was Irwin's first side business, outside Northwestern Bag Company. Though he was never active in the company's daily operations, he was a strong, behind-the-scenes operator and large shareholder.

Within months it was clear that our Sonny's discount store concept couldn't stand on its own and the only chance of success was through Norco Oil. We shifted gears fast to focus on building or acquiring gas stations and stocking them with merchandise. Showing revenue growth with a newly public company was crucial, so we had to be nimble. We added thirteen stations in Wisconsin through an acquisition, began scouting locations, and started building more stations on the fly. We showed a profit, but we were never in the same league with SuperAmerica and Holiday. They put big money into their fancy gas stations and stores, planned them, and built them carefully. We were the upstarts.

LIVING LARGER

Irwin convinced me to become president and CEO of Norco Oil Corporation. All of a sudden I was the twenty-nine-year-old top dog of a publicly traded company that was about to expand into oil wells.

Here's how it happened. Irwin struck up a conversation with two guys, Mel Unger and Irv Green, one day at the Jewish Community Center in the Minneapolis suburb of St. Louis Park. One man had a home in Manhattan and the other in Palm Springs, but they were Canadian businessmen. I don't know how they happened to land in Minnesota.

Unger and Green were investors and promoters who had recently bought control of a Wyoming public company traded on the Canadian stock exchange called Pronghorn. They told Irwin about Pronghorn's oil and gas wells in Wyoming, North Dakota, and Ohio, and described their jade deposits in Wyoming. Irwin was intrigued.

Unger, Green, and Jacobs talked about merging Pronghorn and Norco Oil with Norco as the surviving entity. Unger and Green wanted access to the U.S. stock exchange, and the easiest way to do that was to sell Pronghorn to an American OTC-traded company like Norco.

With the merger complete, Unger and Green owned ninety-five percent of the surviving company, Norco. By doing that, they could trade their stock in the U.S., even though this was a Canadian company. Because they owned a majority of Norco, they were considered insiders and they couldn't trade their stock without full disclosure.

But they got around that by keeping their shares in their Canadian brokerage firm's name, instead of their own. Of course, they weren't visibly involved in the affairs of Norco. Nor was Irwin; he was a minority partner. I was president, CEO, and COO of Norco, and the sole front man. The arrangement felt a little like smoke and mirrors to me, but I took full advantage of the power I had.

I got to be a big shot, with my stock traded on the OTC exchange and a board of directors from the "who's who" of Minneapolis. I wore my three-piece suits, tapped my unlimited expense account, and had a full bar in my private office. Norco had all the right advisers: Lindquist & Vennum, a highly respected law firm with a record of public service, and Arthur Young & Company, old-line accountants. We banked with First National. Everything on the surface was right, but the underpinnings of Norco Oil were questionable.

The business scenario matched my life—looking good on the outside, but shaky inside. As my career pace quickened, so did my dependence on food, alcohol, cigarettes, and diet pills.

JADE ... AND JADED

Norco's twenty-some service stations with convenience stores were company owned and operated and carried the North Star brand of gas. We were in the Twin Cities and small towns like Litchfield, Staples, and Willmar, Minnesota; Madison and Friendship, Wisconsin; and Mayville, North Dakota. I hired a manager to oversee those operations.

I spent my time traveling often in leased Lear jets to Ohio, North Dakota, and Wyoming, checking on our thirty-some gas and oil wells and selling partnerships in new wells. The cost was about $100,000 to drill a well in 1970, and Irwin, as well as some of the big names in the Minneapolis business scene, bought into the partnerships. Like the successful magazine and Christmas Seals salesman of my youth, I could sell partnerships with ease. Of course, every time we struck oil or found natural gas, a glowing press release was issued, the news appeared in papers, and our stock went up a few dollars a share.

I flew to Palm Springs and Manhattan, keeping Unger and Green up-to-speed on the company's progress. As our stock went up, I knew Unger and Green were unloading their holdings through the Canadian stock market. I understood their game, but I was playing my own game that fed all of my addictions.

Then, there were the jade mines—some fifty-six claims that Pronghorn originally owned. We had 500,000 pounds of rock stored in a warehouse in Riverton, Wyoming, waiting to be sorted and studied. We hired the top geologist from the University of Minnesota, to examine our stake; and I went along. I impressed him with our operation, and he published a report saying we had both gem-quality stones and commercial grade that just might be the largest deposit in the world. Worth up to one billion dollars. That got us attention. The news even appeared on the front page of *Women's Wear Daily*, the bible of America's fashion industry. In reality, our stake was semi-precious jade, similar to agate, used in making costume jewelry. It was not the highest quality "jadeite" found in China.

More Lear jet trips followed to Wyoming. More first-class tickets to Manhattan and Palm Springs. More head-expanding, private consults with Irwin, our lawyers, accountants, and blue-chip advisers. More partying and drinking with my business pals. More positive press on local and national business pages.

Within a year of the geologist's assessment of our claim, we

Mom and Dad with
Mom's parents and Mom's
sister Connie

Mom on her
Shetland pony

Mom and Dad on
their wedding day,
November 30, 1932

Grandpa and Grandma Nordstrand, Grandma Swanson, and Grandpa's dog on the farm in Ellsworth, Wisconsin

My older brother Dennis with me on the farm

Dad, my brother Dennis, with Mom holding me in 1939

Dad and his brother Art

My Ellsworth High School
graduation picture

My Army Reserve
ID Card

Me in front of my home fuel delivery truck in 1961.

Me working at North Star gas station 1964

Me as president of Norco Oil Company 1969

Jennie and John with me at home in South Minneapolis 1971

My dad working on the Auto Stop gas station
in River Falls, Wisconsin

At my desk at SSG Corporation in
Hudson, Wisconsin, 1974

Aboard the Oil Slick: (L–R) Fred Bennett, me,
and John P. O'Malley

Neil McGraw, Paul Montgomery, and John Peterson with me
in St. Maarten for our first sailing trip

Anne Marie in front of the Anne Marie 2, 1984

developed a new partnership called Majestic Jade Company, jointly owned by Norco Oil and Felco Jewel Industries, Inc. of New York. We agreed to provide the raw jade; and Felco managed our plant in Albuquerque where local Indian artists designed and made the jade products including jewelry, tile, bowls, vases, decorative boxes ... even tombstones.

Before long, the kid from Ellsworth, Wisconsin, was on Wall Street in a floor-to-ceiling glass conference room overlooking the Statue of Liberty, the East River, and New York Harbor, selling our jade to a group of elegantly dressed morticians. Lending credibility was our expert geologist.

My next stop was a pitch to Wall Street stock analysts where I promoted Norco Oil.

Back home, I sold more oil partnerships, knowing full well that initial production on an oil well always hits a higher volume to start and usually tapers off with time. Sure, the details of production were all in the fine print, but the hype was starting to get to me. I didn't believe that all the projections we made about oil production could be sustained. We were going too far. I wanted to be a high flyer, but this scheme was going to crash and I'd be a fatality. On top of that, I wasn't being rewarded enough for the huge risks I was taking.

I had to stop the train. I had to get off. Norco Oil was a house of cards, and I was head of the household. I had created a life of luxury and shady deals built with other people's money. Had money become my "higher power"? My personal life was toxic: overeating, drinking to blackouts, compensating with diet pills, driving myself unmercifully. By then, I had a wife and two young children at home. My life felt out of control on a high-speed roller coaster, but you wouldn't know it. I knew I had to get off or self-destruct.

THREE

SECRETS CARVE A CHASM

LOVE AT FIRST SIGHT

I was thirty years old, and what did I know? How to put cash in my pocket. How to work a deal and come out on top. How to con disreputable doctors out of diet pills and hide my lust for sweets.

What did I know about love? Zip. I wasn't even sure what it meant to love my wife. In the three years since marrying Sharon, we'd tried to have a baby. She wanted one, but I could wait. My business was taking off and taking me over. I worked marathon days, often followed by dinner and drinks with Jim, Len, and other friends. I'd never heard the term "workaholic," but I was one.

Despite our continuing efforts, Sharon and I just couldn't conceive. I wasn't worried much about it, but something was wrong. We went to doctors, and they checked us out. I passed, but they said Sharon had irregular ovulation and unpredictable periods that made conception harder. Neither of us knew much about sex. We were young, inexperienced, and awkward together.

Finally Sharon suggested adoption. She didn't want to wake up ten years later, childless at forty, and be too old to adopt. The idea was a relief to me. Deep down, I thought I was too flawed; I didn't want to pass on my genes. Adoption was preferable to creating someone like me.

We had the home visits and the paperwork, the counseling, and due diligence by the Children's Home Society. Then the waiting began.

I will never forget May 1968.

Summer came early to Minnesota, and our little South Minneapolis home near Lake Harriet glowed with warm, morning sunlight. The doorbell rang and I answered it. Suddenly, I was staring into the dark eyes of this tiny baby, a seven-pound miracle wrapped in blankets and cuddled by the adoption caseworker. Her biological mom was a medical student who was also adopted. She wanted to pursue her career, and she believed a loving, adoptive couple was a better option for her infant daughter. Our little girl was just three pounds when she was born prematurely and had lived in a foster home since she was a few days old.

I stepped over the threshold and reached for my sweet-smelling, radiant baby girl. We named her Jennifer Lee. A shiver ran through me. *This little person. Is. Mine. Mine to care for. Mine to protect. Mine to raise and nurture. Mine to love.* The feeling was instantaneous and totally new.

Jennie. Not born of my flesh, but born in my heart. This was the first time in my thirty years that I felt total and unconditional love.

I'LL DRINK TO THAT

I had met Sharon Naslund in 1964, just after I left my mentor, John O'Malley, and joined Oskey Brothers Petroleum to head their new gas station division. I was attending an oil convention in downtown Minneapolis and inevitably wound up drinking at the Hilton hotel bar. Sharon was out for the evening with girlfriends. I was immediately attracted to her. She was cute and fun. She laughed at my jokes and drank almost as much as I did.

Sharon was a small town girl from Alexandria, Minnesota, whose dad was a liquor salesman. She worked as a lab technician in the downtown Minneapolis Medical Arts Building and lived in a tiny apartment in South Minneapolis. Sharon was a few years younger than me. We hit it off (the alcohol helped), and I followed up.

We immediately started dating—drinks and dinners, some I couldn't remember. Our courtship floated in Jack Daniels and Chivas Regal. I had added alcohol abuse to my inventory of addictions, and sometimes I had blackouts: periods when I talked, paid the tab, drove, and functioned "normally." The memory lapses were a sure sign of advancing addiction, but I ignored it. Like my dad, I was a binge drinker; I picked up the first drink and kept going until I was good and drunk. Sharon blacked out the first time she drank. Her dad was a verbally abusive, controlling guy, so Sharon didn't trust men and she couldn't express her feelings easily. Our conversations were superficial. She wanted so much to be liked. We were carbon copies.

I described my growing gas station venture to Sharon and told her that any woman who married me would be an "oil widow" because I spent so much time traveling the circuit, supervising my stations, and collecting the receipts.

Within a year I proposed. Most of my friends were getting married, and I thought it was the right thing to do. We had a big wedding on November 14, 1965, in a Catholic church; we honeymooned in Acapulco over Thanksgiving and settled in a duplex on Grand Avenue in South Minneapolis. Soon, we bought our first home at 43rd and Colfax, and I set up my business office there.

The scene was tidy and comfortably conventional. I hoped this new family life would be the opposite of my own in Ellsworth. But how could it be? Sharon and I had great fun together as a newly-married couple, but I was still eating to excess, abusing diet pills, gambling when I could, and working like a fiend. Our weekends as a young, married couple revolved around hard drinking and card games with friends from (would you believe it?) the Episcopal church.

Americans set records for alcohol and cigarette consumption in 1965, and Sharon and I helped raise the average, especially at our church parties. Though we rarely drank at home on weekdays, I often had three-martini business lunches with Jim Emison and others—making plans.

All that drinking led to sexual indiscretions. After all, I reasoned, proponents of open marriage sold sexual freedom in the early 1960s, too. A little fling on the side was nothing unusual back then for many. George Burns and Gracie Allen, the radio and TV comics, appeared to be the only devoted, married couple we knew.

LAND OF LINCOLNS

After I left Oskey Brothers and started my own venture, Sharon helped with bookkeeping and Larry Hopkins, my co-worker from the O'Malley days, set up my gas station accounting system. After Martin

Luther King Jr's assassination in 1968, someone threatened to blow up our gas station on the north side because we only had white employees. Sharon got phone threats at home.

Clueless, I drove around in my fiftieth anniversary Lincoln Continental Silver Edition from one gas station to the other, checking on the business, and picking up the receipts. I was a perfect target for harassment.

At a stop light one night I rolled a little before a full stop and heard a bang on the hood of my car. I looked out and saw a couple of black kids lying in the street. *Did I knock them over?* They didn't seem hurt. I was immediately surrounded, and I didn't know what to do. Scared, I rolled down the window and offered a one hundred dollar bill, and one of the guys snarled, "That's not nearly enough."

I cranked my window back up, put my car in low gear, and slowly rolled through the gathering crowd. I got out of there as fast as I could. At home, I called the police to tell them what happened. I wasn't absolutely sure the kids were okay. The cop's answer was cavalier: "Hey, mister," he said, "thanks for the call, but the only time we take action is if somebody's shooting."

That Lincoln raised a lot of eyebrows, especially when three identical Silver Editions parked outside Turk's Restaurant in Hayward, Wisconsin. My buddies, Jim and Len at Oskey Brothers, joined me at the popular roadhouse decorated with Turkish kitsch and walls papered with signed photos of celebrities and wannabes. That night, someone alerted the nearest police station. The anonymous caller was convinced that three, spotless Lincoln Continentals, parked side by side, could only mean the mafia.

I was living large. The car was a status symbol. So were the tailored suits, vintage scotch, and cigars at petroleum conventions. I had a north woods cabin that I picked up cheap. I built a huge, 400-square-foot deck overlooking Lake Namakagon and turned the cabin into a gathering spot for friends. In those days, I did nothing small.

That's why, when Irwin Jacobs came along, I was ripe for becoming the boy-wonder at Norco Oil. The role was perfect for me. Norco upped the ante. More money. More flash. More spin. Selling oil and gas partnerships with questionable returns. Hawking jade tombstones to upscale morticians. Rationalizing the stock shenanigans of two slippery Canadian businessmen.

I was leading two lives: the high flyer in business and the middle-class husband living in a modest home, who reliably mowed his lawn on weekends—and adopted a baby girl.

MY SEVEN-POUND MIRACLE

That day in 1968, when I met Jennifer Lee, was my first glimpse of pure love. At first I couldn't believe what I was feeling.

Children's Home Society had only brought Jennie to us for a brief visit that first time. They told us they would take her away for the evening, so we could reflect on our decision. But I didn't want her to leave. It hurt to say good-bye, even after knowing her for only thirty minutes. I ached until she came home for good. Sharon and I threw all our energy into being model parents.

But my energy was depleted—by the duplicitous deals at Norco Oil, by the heavy drinking, by the delicate balance I maintained with just enough alcohol, sweets, and carbs to maintain the sugar high I needed to function. At my peak, I packed the pounds onto my six-foot-one frame. Then, I'd diet and fast to drop a quick twenty. At 260 pounds I didn't look obese. I just looked big. I lied about all of it:

overeating, heavy drinking, diet pills, fasts. I kept it all secret, along with the insidious shame that served as the backdrop of my life.

My daughter Jennie was two years old when Sharon and I decided to adopt again in 1970. John was born December 11. When this chubby little boy-bundle arrived at our door with his Children's Home Society caseworker, it happened all over again. I immediately fell in love. Again, they gave us the night to think it over. Of course we wanted him! Sharon and I were both instantly dazzled by our children.

We moved our family across the street into a slightly larger home so Jennie and John could have their own rooms. The purchase was easy. With my Norco Oil income and a well-abused expense account, our little family had all we ever needed. Sharon didn't have to work outside the home.

AFFAIRS TO REMEMBER

But our marriage was unraveling. To be frank, I was "married" to my business. And when I wasn't working, being a good dad was my top priority. Sharon and I were distant and uncommunicative. We tiptoed around each other and tried to keep the peace.

On one of those countless three-martini lunches with my friend Jim, we landed at the Camelot Restaurant in Bloomington—a swinging place in those days, even at lunchtime. Models in provocative outfits sashayed around the tables while we devoured porterhouse steaks and baked potatoes loaded with gobs of sour cream and melted butter. The scene triggered every craving I had for food, sex, alcohol, power.

I met a former Miss Minnesota, a model in the luncheon show. We started drinking and ended up at the Edgewater Inn. The affair lasted a few years. I visited her once or twice a week at the little house she shared with her young son. We went to Las Vegas and gambled a few times. We had fun together and talked easily. I realized I must not be half bad if "a model" was attracted to me. That didn't square with the low self-esteem I hid: *how could a beautiful woman want me?* I was confused by—but thrilled with—the attention. But a single off-limits liaison was not enough. I made many late afternoon phone calls to her and to others, sitting in my office at Norco in St. Louis Park, my hand on the phone, a Scotch in the other.

In the meantime, Sharon came home drunk one night and admitted having affairs of her own. I didn't challenge her, and she seemed not to care about my own less-than-secret liaisons. Both of us were guilty of betrayal; both of us were rejected, lying to ourselves and hiding our pain. Sharon drank away her sadness and found replacements for me. I had turned to my addictions. Our secrets had carved a chasm between us.

Sharon's drinking evolved into full-fledged addiction, though I didn't fully face it. I came home one afternoon to find the wallpaper burning in our living room. A wastebasket had caught fire, John and Jennie were in the house, and Sharon wasn't there. Even then, I minimized Sharon's drinking. I wrote off the fire as an accident, not the result of an alcoholic blackout. *How could I confront Sharon when I was doing the same things?* We were a replay of the heart-wrenching movie, *The Days of Wine and Roses*, with a few extra marital partners.

HITTING BOTTOM

Sharon called my Norco office in tears one weekday morning. "I can't live like this anymore," she told me. "I'm an alcoholic. I just called

56

the Alcoholics Anonymous hotline, and there's someone coming over to talk to me."

By the time I got home, a recovering alcoholic from A.A. was sitting in our living room doing a "12-Step call." She told Sharon her own story, and with each painful detail, Sharon saw herself in the narrative. Daily drinking, nips in the morning to mend a hangover, forgotten evenings, suffocating shame. Alcohol had been Sharon's refuge and relief for years, but alcohol had turned on her. Alcohol was a malevolent force with a chilling goal: illness and death.

That was the first time I heard the term "alcoholic."

Sharon entered residential treatment at St. Mary's Hospital in Minneapolis that same afternoon. My sister Gail helped me care for Jennie and John during the twenty-eight days of Sharon's program stay. I saw myself as the heroic father, keeping all the balls in the air—a victim of my wife's illness.

Oddly, I felt a certain excitement during that crisis. Relief, too. Sharon's alcoholism was something I could name and help "fix." I jumped into problem-solving, getting to know Sharon's therapist and caseworker and going to Al-Anon meetings. Sharon was a "project" I could pour my energies into. I had hope. But even though I immersed myself in learning about alcoholism and co-dependency (that obsession with "fixing" other people), I never honestly examined my own addictions. None of it applied to me. *Denial?* You bet.

When Sharon completed her treatment, we began marriage counseling and moved to a new home on Proehl's Trail in Hudson, Wisconsin. This was a fresh start for us. (In the recovery community, they call it "a geographic," a superficial change that doesn't address the real issues.) Our new home was closer to western Wisconsin—the focus of a new venture materializing in my imagination.

I had stopped drinking to support Sharon's recovery, but it wasn't such a personal sacrifice. I found it easier than giving up my three-pack-a-day cigarette habit one year earlier when little Jennie said, "Daddy, cigarettes will hurt you." (The U.S. Surgeon General had just issued a report declaring that cigarettes were dangerous to human health.) In the first few weeks of giving up nicotine, I had powerful cravings twenty-four hours a day, seven days a week. I needed to keep my hands busy, so I remodeled the basement, turning it into a family room in a matter of days. By the fourth week, I finally felt better. I even recognized the advantages of not having my pockets loaded with half-used matchbooks and my clothes scarred with cigarette burns.

Besides, I had high-octane sugar to carry me through withdrawal from nicotine *and* alcohol. Now I "used" caffeine, diet pills, and gambling. I may have appeared "sober" to the outside world, but I sure wasn't clean.

SEEING IS BELIEVING

Sharon's personal crisis forced me to think. I knew I had to get off the roller coaster I was living at Norco Oil. I had already visualized the details of my new business, and my daughter had invented a name for it.

I often took Jennie with me on rounds of the gas stations Norco owned. Each time we approached a stop sign, Jennie shouted, "That says 'stop,' Daddy." In her little girl garble, it sounded like "Auto Stop" to me.

While I mowed my lawn, I drew mental pictures: where the Auto Stop gas stations would be, how to make them unique and more competitive, what my big office would look like—even down to the

Italian tile, fireplace, gas pumps out front, and a "cashier's window" where my receptionist would sit. I had learned the power of visualization years before when I envisioned a network of stations for Oskey Brothers; I saw myself leveraging Norco's oil partnerships into a mega-business.

Years later, when I talked about the power of visualization with friends, I was often told, "You should write a book about it." When I finally got into recovery from my addictions, I understood that visualization was not *my* special gift, but God's way of staying anonymous. I also realized that I squandered that gift when my addictions kept me numb and unable to discern God's influence on my life.

Auto Stop became reality on June 20, 1971, when I drove back to the Twin Cities alone from our cabin. I arrived at a tiny, Wisconsin town called Siren—just a few buildings, a tavern, a small grocery store, and a closed Holiday gas station on Highway 35. Holiday had already opened a new station down the street, and its cast-off property didn't even have a "for sale" sign. I stopped at the grocery to get my supply of sugar, carbs, and caffeine; then I walked over to that closed station and asked a guy who was loading some discarded equipment, "Who owns this?"

"My brother."

"Where's your brother?"

"In Chicago."

That same night I called the owner in Chicago and asked what he wanted for his property. He said $7,500 and I quickly agreed. That was my first Auto Stop location. Years later, Art Erickson, one of the owners of Holiday Stores, told me that if he knew what I was going to do with his old store in Siren, he would have burned it down!

BUCKING THE TREND

I couldn't have a station like everyone else. I had to have a defining difference. I was aware of self-service gas stations in the South and West, but there were none in western Wisconsin. In fact, self-serve stations were illegal in Minnesota for safety reasons. Standing squarely behind that law was "big oil"—companies including Standard, Mobil, and Shell, who opposed self-service because it introduced lower prices and the self-service business model challenged big oil's own retail approach.

People in the Midwest were accustomed to cheap, plentiful gas and stations where an attendant filled your car with gas, checked your oil, and washed your windshields. These stations sold gas, oil, auto supplies, and repairs. Most had vending machines selling cigarettes, soft drinks, and candy, usually in a cramped, dusty space next to the tires waiting for patches.

We were the first self-service station in the Upper Midwest, and my competitive advantage was price. By pumping their own gas and paying cash, motorists got more gallons for their money. Later, I added convenience foods and snacks.

My dad, who was known as "Pa" after he became a grandfather, retired from farming in the summer of 1970. He was, once again, battling depression. One of my motivations for starting my company was to give him something to do. I hired Pa to help me remodel the station in Siren. I named the company that owned my Auto Stop stores after my dad. I called it The Alvin Corporation. Though I guessed the name would please him, it did not. I rarely succeeded in winning his approval, though I kept trying.

The Siren Auto Stop was a building we boarded up on the front and installed a small cashier's window in the kitchen, similar to a Dairy Queen. The interior looked like a nicely appointed mobile home with one bedroom and a living room complete with a TV. In front, we installed gas pumps, a bright red-and-yellow canopy, and Auto Stop billboards with lettering visible almost a mile away: "Save," "Self-Serve," "Gas for Less." Compared to our competition, our store had the razzle-dazzle of a traveling circus.

I'd heard about the practice in the South of having live-in operators, but I had never seen it in the Midwest. We were the first. I hired a retired couple to live at the station and handle the gas business. They had free housing (better than they had before), and it was easy work. The cashier's window became the center of their social life with regular customers and friends visiting. Auto Stop offered a financial supplement to their Social Security payments.

That first summer we sold our gas—regular and ethyl—for 26.9 cents per gallon, five cents below our competition. We did so much business; it took two years to introduce credit cards. I had planned to use credit cards immediately, but I didn't want to saddle our retired couple with more responsibility during that chaotic opening week. We were going great guns. Even so, our competition snickered and thought we'd go away.

The Siren station began generating $5,000-a-month profit, and that helped quickly pay down my $30,000 building cost. We had minimal overhead: my sister Gail, who managed the company's books from our family home in Ellsworth; myself; and, soon, Larry Hopkins from Norco Oil. After six months, Don Dahlstrom, a seasoned oil man, joined us, too.

I drove around Wisconsin with Don, scouting new locations for Auto Stop stations in 1971. He followed me in his car and witnessed my sugar addiction in high gear. I bought ten packages of Wrigley's spearmint gum before our tour began. Every minute or so, Don saw me toss another gum wrapper out the window. I devoured ten packs of gum in less than an hour.

THE BEAUTY OF BANKRUPTCY

A few weeks before opening my Siren station, I told Irwin Jacobs that I wanted out of Norco Oil. I left in September 1971. One of my employees at Norco, took my place. Irwin resisted. He was upset with my decision, and he went on the offensive. I had been the "glue" that held Norco together.

That was a scary time. Had Irwin been successful with his threatened lawsuit, it probably would have cost me my new company. My replacement worked hard to supply Norco's high-powered lawyers with ammunition to use against me. Some of it was true. I *did* abuse my expense account. But I wouldn't admit it, then.

Irwin argued conflict of interest based on my role at Norco and my after-hours formation of Alvin Corporation. My attorney wanted a $50,000 retainer fee upfront—a frightening financial stretch for me.

As it turned out, Norco's house of cards crumbled before any lawsuit got off the ground. Norco declared Chapter 7 bankruptcy. Unlike filing Chapter 11 for business reorganization, the choice of Chapter 7 meant the game was over—liquidation. No more Norco. Their lawyers were left unpaid.

I was spared the anxiety of a protracted lawsuit. Coincidentally, not long after Norco's bankruptcy, an oil shortage hit America and natural gas prices shot up. Returns from Norco's existing gas wells paid off all of the company's waiting creditors, with money left over. One of my best friends, a bankruptcy attorney, reflected that this was the only high-profile case he'd ever seen where a failed company actually became a success in bankruptcy.

STATIONS WITH STAYING POWER

With our family settled into a "comfortable" life in Hudson, Wisconsin, Sharon was active in A.A. and the local arts center, and she was busy with Jennie and John. She struggled to stay sober while I became totally engrossed in my business. Work was my new drug, I couldn't get enough.

By June of 1972, our first thirteen Auto Stop stations were built in prime locations on busy highways: Siren, Ladysmith, Ellsworth, River Falls, Spooner, Barron, downtown Hudson, Tomahawk, Medford, Milltown, Marshfield, Cornell, and Merrill.

Don Dahlstrom scouted new locations and helped supervise the ones we already had. When Don found a prime spot, I acted fast. I drove there the same evening. I looked over the often-closed and locked building, broke in if I had to, checked it out, then found the owner. I'd go to his home, introduce myself, sit down at his kitchen table with my yellow pad, and write a purchase agreement. I took our building plan to the state and set our construction team loose. My pace was manic. I was a whirling dervish high on activity (and my other ever-present addictions).

Pa and I actually built our second Auto Stop in Ladysmith by ourselves, including the petroleum piping. He loved going from town to town (even though he grumbled to me about it). Pa spent the week building a station and commuting home on weekends. I hired a team of plumbers and electricians to travel with us; we added a carpenter to assist Pa.

Meanwhile, my sister Gail, who was fresh out of college, grappled with the complexity of our growing company. She balanced income and outgo, gas purchases and contractor payments.

I managed our cash flow, using leverage. I had enough money to build the Siren station. Revenue from Siren generated enough to finance our second station in Ladysmith. The second financed the third in Ellsworth, and on and on. Before too long, we had enough success to take our financials to community banks for bridge loans. In those days, we even projected our sales at each location for the following day, wrote a check for that amount, deposited it, and the bank considered it collected cash. We knew what to expect, and gas prices didn't fluctuate.

When we built the station in Ellsworth and cut our gas prices to compete with Pa's neighbors, he wasn't so proud of The Alvin Corporation name that I had chosen to honor him. He was skeptical of my rapid growth, even though he enjoyed his role in building the stations. He convinced me to change my company's name; he wanted nothing to do with the enterprise. I re-named my company SSG Corporation (Self-Service Gas), which nicely underscored our competitive difference.

Every one of our Auto Stop stations had a story, often colorful. Just after we finished building our Marshfield station, I got a call from our manager. "We have a little problem with our canopy," she told me. At closing time, a drunk man left the tavern across the street, climbed into his dumptruck, missed the highway, and barreled into our station driveway. He hit the wrong lever in his cab and the back of the dumptruck flipped up. He was going thirty miles per hour when he collided with our Auto Stop canopy—just twenty feet from the place where our station operators were sleeping. The canopy posts were more than twelve inches square, and solid steel. That after-hours marauder moved the entire canopy four feet and tested the resolve of our senior citizen managers.

Every one of our senior operators was dedicated and committed to the new venture. They needed little supervision, and they were having fun watching the business grow right in front of them. Of our first thirteen Auto Stop stations, twelve remained strong producers and the existing buildings were eventually rebuilt and expanded by acquiring an adjacent lot or home. The only station that didn't last was Milltown. The state purchased it to widen the road. Our little store was replaced with a park bench.

I called those months from June 1971 through June 1972, "the first magnificent year." SSG Corporation was truly a "pioneer," and one of the few original self-service gas companies still thriving in 2010.

COMMISERATING WITH CHRYSLER

The thrill of growth and success was quickly consumed by fear when the world as I knew it changed forever in the summer of 1972. SSG's future was suddenly in serious doubt. I was visiting our Milltown location when Gail called me and said that President Nixon—himself embroiled in the Watergate scandal—had announced a strict allocation system for oil. An oil shortage was already apparent in America. Before long the Arabs announced an oil embargo against the U.S., Western Europe, and Japan in retaliation for supporting Israel. The Arabs' cut-off triggered an energy crisis in the entire industrialized world.

America's allocation system was to be managed by a new government agency called the Federal Energy Office (FEO). Not only did they determine how much fuel every company received, but they also dictated the profit margins we earned each month. The FEO set allocation amounts based on purchases a company made the previous year, so we became a casualty of the calendar. Because we were a new company and we didn't have purchases for the first half of 1971, we were at risk of being shut off by our suppliers. Suppliers wanted to sell to us, but the law wouldn't allow that.

The day after Gail told me the news, I flew to Washington, D.C. We only had four days to solve the crisis before we'd run out of gas.

I came prepared. I had a petition making a strong case for our allocation, written by my attorney, Don Campbell. I had Washington contacts supplied by Jim Emison, in case I needed extra leverage. The Federal Energy Office looked like an old, converted warehouse. Borrowed IRS agents sat in that large, open space, surrounded by stacks of paperwork. I waited in the reception area all day with many others in the same fix. I told the guy next to me that if I didn't get a gasoline allocation in four days, my company would be out of business. He said that if he didn't get a fuel oil allocation, his assembly line would close. He was an executive vice president at Chrysler. We were in the same boat.

By about four p.m. that day, I was assigned an agent. I had letters from my two biggest suppliers, Murphy Oil and Northwestern Refining, saying they were willing to supply us, but they couldn't because of the new law. The agent agreed to an emergency allocation of 600,000 gallons a month, equally divided between Murphy and Northwestern. Though it was a lot at the time, the allocation was about eighty percent of what we actually needed. I succeeded through sheer perseverance, much like my mother persevered quietly and confidently.

The whole experience in Washington was a rush of its own. My addictions worked in my favor. Addicts thrive on what experts call "terminal uniqueness." We think we are just a little smarter than everyone else, just a little stronger than everyone else. That certainty about myself propelled me forward and helped me make a compelling case. As good as Chrysler.

The agent typed the allocation order into a wordgram (a bureaucrat's version of a telegram), and I talked him into letting me *personally* mail the notice to our suppliers. In my excitement, I mixed the messages up and put Northwestern's allocation confirmation in Murphy's envelope and vice versa. Everyone got a kick out of that.

WHAT REBATE CHECK?

We were back in business. With our emergency allocation, we had enough gasoline to get by, but we could have sold a lot more. I made several trips back to Washington that year, looking for ways to get additional allocations. I had to change my thinking from "how to *sell* gasoline" to "how to *get* gasoline." The Federal Energy Office was on its way to becoming the largest of all federal agencies.

Our competitors ran out of gasoline as waiting lines lengthened and motorists fumed. One night in 1972, I had dinner with a friend and saw a TV report saying that the only gas station in the metropolitan area still open at eight P.M. was a station in Hudson, Wisconsin. Good God, it was my station! My friend and I drove as fast as we could to the station only to find more than one hundred cars forming a line around the block. Our tanks were half full, but I was afraid we'd run out. I stood in the street, trying to wave new customers away, knowing I wouldn't have enough. Each person had a hard luck story about needing to get to work in the morning.

Gas prices soared from about thirty cents to nearly seventy cents a gallon in about two months that year before the price leveled off. Stations with gas supplies made more money as the prices rose, but the higher prices also slowed demand. Some station operators got into trouble with cash flow, but we were conservative enough to stay whole. Gail and I kept a close eye on our cash.

If we had more control over gasoline distribution, I figured we could protect our continued supply, so I bought three tractor-trailer rigs to transport gas. We painted them in bright colors and they became rolling billboards for Auto Stop. Our drivers helped us keep tabs on our suppliers, too. The truck drivers always heard the industry gossip first. One of them heard that Northwestern Refining had charged more than the amount allowed by the government. Because this happened, our company and others deserved a rebate. Hearing that, I called my representative and friend at Northwestern Refining. He said, "Didn't I tell you that you have to fill out a form requesting the rebate?" No form, no rebate check. I knew nothing of a rebate or a form to fill out. I quickly got an application, completed it, and sent it by courier. It arrived one day before the deadline. We had no idea what rebate, if any, we deserved. Three months later we got a check for $250,000 from Northwestern, a huge amount at that time. For a little company like ours, that helped ease my near-constant cash flow worries.

We later learned that Northwestern's company-owned operation, SuperAmerica, may have been the only one that knew about that rebate form. Apparently any rebates that were not requested by a customer who deserved the funds were reallocated to those who asked.

The fewer the applicants, the more money SuperAmerica kept.

I also had to challenge our other big supplier, Murphy. Murphy was scheduled to give us our gasoline allocation on the 20th of each month, and they bumped the actual delivery to the first of the following month. That way, they had control of 300,000 gallons for their own use for the first month of our allocation and, by waiting until the first of the month when the government adjusted prices, they could probably charge us more. When I realized what was happening, I threatened Murphy with legal action and successfully obtained our allocation on time.

DOWN BY THE RIVER

Back in our sleepy little town, living large on the St. Croix River called for a boat. In 1973, *Oil Slick*, my forty-three-foot Nautilus houseboat, became the first in a succession of my marine love affairs. She was moored just a mile from my office in downtown Hudson. *Oil Slick* was my "clubhouse." I invited customers and friends to join me on the boat. I took great pride in keeping *Oil Slick* shipshape.

My gang of guy friends took trips down the St. Croix, up the Mississippi to the Saint Paul Yacht Club, the Pool and Yacht Club, and on through Lock #1 at the Ford Parkway Bridge to Minneapolis and the Edgewater Inn. Or we cruised down to Red Wing or Lake City, Minnesota, stopped at one of many beaches and finished the tour at the St. Croix Yacht Club. That was the first of many summers that I took a trip all the way down the Mississippi to Iowa. I planned cruises from one party stop to another. We pulled into marinas—all show and bravado, oiled by alcohol and rich food. The whole thing fed my big-shot image.

DOUBLE WHAMMY

There were actually two oil crises—one in 1972 and the second in 1974. The double whammy tumbled America into a deep recession. A big New York Stock Exchange firm failed—the first in twenty-six years—and Congress created the SIPC (Securities Investor Protection Corporation) backed by the U.S. Treasury. Stock market trading volume plummeted; borrowers saw interest rates soar to double digits, and people were scared. A defiant Richard Nixon waved his last good-bye as president on August 9, 1974, when he resigned to avoid impeachment by Congress. The nation breathed a sigh of relief, but we at SSG worried about what would come next.

During the second oil crisis, SSG bought gas stations just to get the additional allocations. In Albert Lea, Minnesota, I gave the gas station property away to a friend because I had no intention of developing it. But we kept the gas allocation. We devised ways to buy additional gasoline in Canada, so SSG was free of Federal Energy Office limitations. I secured a gasoline storage facility in Osceola, Wisconsin, near a train track and had gas transported from Canada by rail. Even with a thirty-cent-per-gallon freight charge, SSG still made money on that gas because prices were so high.

Jim Emison and I courted Saudi sheiks before the Arab oil-producing nations cut off their shipments to the U.S., Western Europe, and Japan in 1973. A consummate deal-maker, Jim had gone to Riyadh in Saudi Arabia to meet with six oil sheiks who seemed open to selling fuel directly to us. There he was, a rogue Midwestern businessman, meeting with these powerful Saudis in a voluminous, air-conditioned tent in the desert, sitting cross-legged on a floor mat, sipping dark Arabian coffee, negotiating quantities, dickering over prices. No need for an Arabic translator, everyone involved spoke fluent English. I was all set to follow-up the agreements that Jim negotiated on a second trip to the Middle East, but the deal fell through when fighting broke out between the Arabs and Israelis and peace talks floundered.

FACING THE UNKNOWN

At home in Hudson, Sharon and I faced new fears. Our son, John, had not yet spoken words beyond limited babytalk. As an infant, he responded to sounds, but by age two, we worried about this delay in his speech. We now began taking him to doctors. Some physicians told us John was just late in developing verbal skills. Others scared us with talk of possible brain damage.

There was no single test to determine deafness. We learned that children can lose their hearing at a young age if they suffer a high fever. One day they're normal, and the next, after being sick with the flu or a cold, they can be deaf. This was assumed to have happened to John. But he was so quick to adapt and respond to interaction, we weren't certain whether he could hear or not. When John was finally diagnosed with deafness six months later, it was a relief to know the truth. He was prescribed hearing aids, about two inches square, connected to cords running to his ears. Sharon made him little T-shirts with tiny pockets for each of the aids.

The day John was fitted for his hearing aids for the first time, I turned on the radio in the car on the way home. He started crying and pulled the cords from his ears. The sudden sound jarred and disrupted his quiet world. The devices provided amplification of the noises around John, but the sounds were not identical to what a hearing person experiences.

He adapted to his hearing aids, albeit slowly at first. His use of language had to begin again as if he were a baby, learning first his name, Mom and Dad, Jennie, puppy, and so on. John's hearing remained limited, but we persevered and he learned quickly. Jennie helped him, too, speaking directly to John and pronouncing words clearly.

ADDICTION TRUMPS INTIMACY

Sharon was a good mother when she could be, but she remained vulnerable to anxiety. She put together only a few weeks at a time of sobriety before anxiety and worry chipped away at her. Anxiety prompts people like us to reach for our drug of choice, and then the drug itself further fuels the anxiety—a vicious cycle. Addiction provides a ready answer for pain: drink it away, drug it away, eat it away. Fill in the verb.

I had just returned from another trip to the Federal Energy Office in Washington in December 1973. When I called home and couldn't get an answer, I stopped at the Decathlon Club and phoned Sharon's therapist. He told me Sharon had just had an appointment with him and she had been drinking. She had left his office with an open bottle in her car. Fortunately, Jennie and John were with a neighbor.

Sharon ended up at the Radisson Hotel, ready to drink herself into oblivion. Fortunately, she called her sponsor and then me. She agreed to go right back to residential treatment that night. Sharon's second round of treatment at St. Mary's, a tough, win-sobriety-at-all-costs program, was like going home for her—familiar and safe. While there, Sharon met Jack, another patient, and their friendship bloomed.

When she returned home after completing treatment in January 1974, Sharon told me she wanted a divorce. I agreed with her readily, though I cried at the kitchen table.

We sat down with the children in the dining room—Jennie was five and John had just turned three. We told them that Mom and Dad wouldn't be living together anymore. I watched Jennie quietly retreat into her pain; tears rolled down her cheeks. John was too young to understand. The initial change in our home life meant I moved into the basement where I had my office. The kids actually found that kind of exciting; both kids seemed to adapt quickly. During the entire transition, Jennie was a rock of stability.

Our divorce process was mercifully short. We didn't argue about anything. I gave Sharon what she wanted, the Hudson house sold quickly, and Sharon bought a nice home in Edina, a Minneapolis suburb, where Jennie and John would live with her. By the summer I was in my own place. We had settled on a flexible schedule so that the kids could be with me frequently during the week and every other weekend.

Our decision to divorce was almost a relief after years of knowing our marriage was virtually dead on arrival. Why? Where there is active addiction, there is *no chance* for intimacy. Our addictions were in charge, effectively pushing both of us out of our marriage.

FOUR

KEEPING A LID ON MY ADDICTION BOX

TIME ON THEIR HANDS

I called them "Mr. and Mrs. Clock." Two, large kitchen clocks, each with an on and off switch, positioned on the wall at the cashier's window of each Auto Stop station. The hour hand pointed to noon. When Mr. (or Mrs.) Senior Citizen Station Operator stepped up to the window to help a customer, he flipped the switch on. When he was finished and went back to his afternoon soap opera, crossword puzzle or nap, he flipped off the switch.

Our stations were open from seven A.M. to ten P.M., and our seniors had lots of time off, but someone always had to be there. At the end of the day, our retired couple filled out their time cards, based on the daily reading of the two clocks. If the clock read five o'clock, it meant he worked five hours. Each couple earned about five hundred dollars a month in addition to the free accommodations. Some of the operators even sold candy, chips, and pop as their own little side businesses.

My clock idea didn't cut it when a federal wage and hour inspector paid us a call in 1975. He told us that a change in the law required SSG to pay our senior citizen operators the minimum hourly wage based on a forty-hour work week.

"But they're not working full time," I said, "not even close. Look at the time cards based on the wall clocks. Besides, when we divide up their hours and calculate their pay, they often make more than the minimum wage already."

No one had seen this kind of operation, and the regulators were confused. They weren't sure how to deal with us. Auto Stop didn't fit their rules, and that made them uneasy.

"Well," our visitor said, "try to figure out how to satisfy the new law or you might be seeing me again."

The clocks worked for a couple years, until some younger employees slapped us with a lawsuit.

BOXED IN

Even though worldwide inflation in the early 1970s caused dramatic cost increases in fuel and food, and economic growth in most industrialized nations sunk to zero. Auto Stop plugged along. We had added five more stations by November 1974, making our grand total eighteen. I never had a long-term plan for the number of stations I might build. I operated on instinct and grabbing the next, big opportunity.

My business life was a heady blend of crises averted (gasoline shortages) and never-before-seen innovation (self-serve and senior operators living in our stations), but my personal life was painful and chaotic. After Sharon and I divorced on April 10, 1974, Pa died, my

Grandma Nordstrand died, and I moved twice in less than two years. If I had a "soul sickness" before, it was chronic and deep now. I had to hold myself together for Jennie and John, for my business, for my employees, for my family, in any way I could.

Pa's death in December 1974 at age sixty-three was inevitable, but tragic nevertheless. His arteries were plugged and his blood vessels collapsed. He suffered multiple heart attacks, and there was nothing to do. No open heart surgery. No bypass procedures. His life of smoking, stress, eating the wrong food, and too much of it, ravaged him. He suffered from the same addictions I had, but he got no help. When I was growing up, no one in my family understood compulsive overeating, depression, or alcoholism. We never even heard the words.

Pa had worked hard on the family farm and his only vacation was one day each year at the state fair. Occasionally, he briefly visited his parents in Missouri, and once he visited my brother Dennis in California. Pa was an intelligent man who followed politics and current affairs closely and knew a little about a lot of subjects. He could carry on a conversation equally well with a laborer or a presidential candidate. But his smarts didn't keep him from slowly killing himself. I am convinced that Pa's early death was caused by the cumulative effects of his addictions. He didn't understand any of it, and he suffered alone. Everyone in our family carried that legacy of fear and sadness with us.

The family gathered for two occasions in December 1974: my sister Gail's marriage to Don Dahlstrom and Pa's funeral—just a couple days apart. The contrast was surreal.

Less than a year later, Olga Nordstrand, my tough Swedish grandmother who survived her husband's suicide and carried on as the family matriarch, died. Grandma Swanson, my mom's doting stepmother, also passed in 1977.

Through it all, I didn't grieve those losses: the end of my marriage, the deaths of Pa and my two grandmas. I simply didn't "feel" like normal people feel. I numbed my pain with food, caffeine, diet pills, and excessive work. Before long, I returned to gambling and drinking.

SUDDENLY SINGLE

My divorce from Sharon fed my low self-esteem. She had wanted out, and I had just gone along with it. She had Jack. That part was embarrassing, but I explained it away to friends and family by pointing to her alcoholism. *Who could blame me for not wanting to live with that?*

Faced with being single in the spring of 1974, I didn't know the script. I still *looked* like a big shot, driving my Lincoln Continental into the parking lot at McKnight Village, a big apartment complex just east of downtown St. Paul. I met the rental agent and told her I wanted to rent an apartment.

"Okay," she said, giving me the once over.

"I'd like it filled with rental furniture, so it's all put together, ready to move in."

"Okay," she said.

"And, by the way," I said, a little sheepishly, "I'll need it soon because I'm getting a divorce."

"No kidding," she said. A poorly veiled smirk. A knowing look.

We made a deal for the apartment, and the next day I left on a cheap weekend trip to Las Vegas. I needed to get away, do a little gambling, and ease the pain of my divorce. Addicts can use any life situation to rationalize their addictive behavior.

I came home from Las Vegas to my new home feeling some relief, even hope about my future. But when I walked into my apartment, I was paralyzed. I hadn't lived alone in a long time. I found all my rented furniture clustered in the middle of the room, toilet paper and paper towels stacked on a table, silverware in boxes, a packaged shower curtain, a waste basket, a plunger.

What in the hell do I do with all this? I stood in the middle of that one-bedroom apartment with its plywood-thin walls and a roll-out couch for the kids.

I started to cry. Then I wanted to eat.

I was pushing 260 pounds again, and my eating was out of control. Binging on huge portions, snacking on pretzels, peanuts, and candy bars. No limits. I hid my fat frame under carefully tailored suits, but it wasn't good enough. I decided I'd better shape up; I had to be presentable to enter the dating scene.

Controlling my weight was harder because I gave up diet pills. I made that decision one day while driving along Interstate 94. I was sick of the hassle, and I dumped my pills out on the roadside near Menomonie, Wisconsin. Frankly, they had become harder to get. These pills were speed, and fewer sleazy doctors were willing to sell a controlled substance. The pills helped me eat less, but I became dependent on them. I needed them to feel halfway normal. When I traveled, the first thing I packed was the pills. If I took more than I should, I was hyper and anxious. It was a tough balancing act. Surprisingly, I struggled through only four days with withdrawal and heavy craving. I was mad at myself for believing I couldn't live without them. I could have dumped them sooner. In reality, I just gave up one addictive substance and turned to others.

Looking back on it now, giving up the diet pills, and attacking my weight problem without them, was the first crack in my wall of denial.

The passing thought that I might be an addict took up a tiny corner in my brain. *After all, my dad was an addict. Maybe it runs in the family?* But that awareness was fleeting. I always had good reasons for overeating. I worked ungodly hours. I was a responsible, single dad. I took care of lots of people. I'd been hurt. I deserved a little pleasure.

I decided to turn my new apartment into a real home—a safe haven for me and my children. I called an old friend from the Episcopal church party gang who had a talent for decorating, and she whipped my little space into shape. Jennie and John often stayed with me, but the times were sometimes hard. John was only three years old, and he railed against his deafness. He often shouted and ranted in sheer frustration. I worried that the whole apartment could hear him. Jennie, still my little rock, tried to calm and comfort her little brother.

Sharon and Jack had an active social schedule, so I saw my children three days a week. I was on good behavior: no binging or drinking in front of them. No dates. I kept my relationship with them in a protected "box" containing the best version of normal I could create. I put my successful, growing business (and reputation) in a separate box, and I hid my addictions in a third box where no one could see them.

I continued to help Sharon after our divorce by paying for more alcohol treatment and counseling, though it was never successful. It is a mystery to me why some people receive the miracle of recovery and others don't. I do not think that recovery depends solely on willpower or the desire to stop drinking, alone.

After years of unabated cigarette smoking, as well as continuing alcohol abuse, Sharon was diagnosed with cancer and began chemotherapy. In 2009 chemo treatments Sharon was undergoing for cancer brought on a debilitating stroke and a series of heart attacks. Just before she died on August 17, God gave her a full week of sobriety and the unique opportunity to make amends and say good-bye to her children and grandchildren.

WEIGHT WATCHERS SUPERSTAR

I joined Weight Watchers. I was the only guy at my first meeting with twenty women in a strip shopping center near the 3M headquarters. We each weighed in, and the leader reported our results. Lots of hoots and applause. I remember beaming when I stood up to bask in the "attaboys" after reporting my first ten-pound loss.

I was among people who understood food cravings and the shame linked to binging.

I followed the Weight Watchers prescribed diet, and I loved those meetings because I got lots of attention. I was determined to become a Weight Watchers superstar, and I didn't disappoint. I lost eighty pounds in twelve months. *Could it be this easy?*

I exercised on a small, round trampoline in my apartment for twenty minutes a day; then I started running to help drop the pounds faster. First, just a half mile, then three miles, then five miles every day. I had joined the Decathlon Club in Bloomington as a charter member with my friend Jim Emison, so I pursued my daily workouts without fail. The Decathlon was an upscale gym, restaurant, and meeting place for people who fit my profile: successful, entrepreneurial, savvy networkers, people who fancied themselves the movers and shakers of the Twin Cities; more upbeat and younger than those stodgy, old-money folks who populated the downtown Minneapolis Club and its venerable twin in St. Paul.

The Decathlon was my clubhouse and second home. That's where I met several lifelong friends. These men became my "fraternity" and my extended family. Over three decades, we went on fishing trips to the Northwest Territories and other parts of Canada, annual ski treks to Vail and Aspen, and sailing trips on my boat in the Caribbean. These guys got to know me very well, including my character defects. They tell me I'm a hyper, high achiever, a perfectionist. I can be intolerant and impatient. I have a heightened sense of duty. I'm compulsive in virtually every area of my life. Well, they're right. One of my greatest gifts in life is a circle of caring friends who will tell me the truth and love me in spite of my flaws.

IN PURSUIT OF THE RUSH

My running route from McKnight Village apartments took me by a new condominium under construction on Upper Afton Road. I needed a better haven for myself and my kids. Bigger, more private, classier. I put down money and bought the second unit at Connemara Condominiums in 1975. My architect friend from Hudson, Elliot Anderson, introduced me to Kathy Young, an interior decorator, who stepped in and turned my space into a contemporary showcase of chrome and glass furniture and fixtures—a popular style at the time.

I was so proud of the final product that I threw a party for my neighbors. I was back in shape, well under two hundred pounds, and feeling high on my new life. I picked up my first drink in months, and I didn't stop until I was drunk.

Addicts have a unique way of thinking, "If some is good, more is better." In those days, gambling junkets for high rollers and wannabes were popular, and I signed up. I flew once or twice a month—sometimes more—to Las Vegas, later adding Monte Carlo, San Juan, even Aruba to my destinations. I always traveled on a large private jet, a 747 or 737. I was the guest of people who planned these junkets and paid all the first-class accommodations. All I had to do was gamble. My "line" (minimum) was $5,000. Sometimes I lost it all, sometimes I won double.

The money was secondary. Vegas was my ticket to unlimited eating and drinking. The rush of winning was intoxicating, too. That feeling came on fast as my luck changed. I'd be down to $5,000 and make a fast comeback. My adrenaline pumped. Sweat surfaced. I had laser-like focus. I still remember specific hands and certain dealers, especially what a dealer said when he folded and I won.

After each trip, I stored my hundred dollar bills in a safe deposit box for the next time. I was addicted to the action and the heady feeling of being "somebody." Those were the days when Vegas was hot. Frank Sinatra and his "rat pack," including Sammy Davis, Jr., Dean Martin, and Peter Lawford were the resident royalty. They set the pace for drinking, womanizing, and the extravagant life. The rest of us tried to be like them.

Being treated like a big shot supplied its own high: "Mr. Nordstrand, here's a front row seat for tonight's show," or "Mr. Nordstrand, you have a $50,000 credit line with us." Recognition was becoming my "higher power," too.

There were plenty of beautiful, available women, lots of food and drinking in those days. I had a fast and reliable way to forget and not feel. I was a high roller. An entrepreneur. Single. Cocky. Available.

I wasn't seeing a woman during what I now call my "playboy years." Occasionally, I connected with my former girlfriend (Miss Minnesota), but I was never serious enough about her to pursue a permanent relationship. The women I hung around with were part of the gambling and drinking scene. They were beautiful, but there wasn't one I'd ever introduce to Jennie or John. My drinking blackouts returned, so I don't remember all the details of those encounters. (I didn't know I could have sex without being drunk.) My slender physique and money made me attractive. Though I was still inexperienced with women, I knew how to charm them, and it came in handy.

Some of the women I met were lovely girls from small towns who worked for the casinos. They wanted the glitter of this fantasy life to rub off on them. I'm sorry I never took the time to really get to know them. I was totally self-indulgent.

MANAGING THE 'LOOK GOOD'

Keeping my life in separate isolated "boxes" was hard work. I was still the successful, hardworking Hudson, Wisconsin, businessman. And, I was the charming, well-dressed, big spender on gambling trips. (I thought everybody got drunk on airplanes.) Most important, I was the dutiful, attentive dad: welcoming Jennie and John to my home at Connemara, helping with Indian Guides projects, attending their sports events, taking them to Disneyland, and cruising on the river aboard my boat, the *Oil Slick*.

I was the typical addict, keeping secrets and living separate, parallel lives to protect my addictive habits. The public version that most people saw looked normal: having a good job and a home, paying bills on time, volunteering in the community. The other life remained hidden: the life of addiction, blackouts, lies, manipulation, and the first thought of the day—how will I get my drug? How will I get enough? How can I hide what I'm doing?

I've heard people in recovery say they "had to get rid of their 'look-good,' in order to feel good." My "look-good" was getting harder to manage. Active addiction is like the guy who used to appear on Ed

Sullivan's TV show. He spun plates on a stick. What made it harder and harder was adding more and more plates. My multiple addictions were those plates.

My primary drug was still food, especially sugar and carbs, and I kept my weight in check by fasting after frequent binges. I worked out even more. I was an "exercise bulimic" who overdid my workouts for the same reason bulimic people vomit to lose calories. Sometimes I accelerated my body's purging with laxatives.

I had terrifying "fat dreams," believing that I gorged all night and gained forty pounds. Waking up in a sweat, I was exhausted but relieved to discover it was only a dream. Even after years of recovery from compulsive overeating, I still have those dreams, the same way alcoholics dream that they've gone on a bender, only to wake up totally sober. We never fully recover from our disease, and as they say in 12-Step groups, addiction is "cunning, baffling, and powerful." I would add "patient."

From 1974 to 1977, my playboy life accelerated and so did my addictive behavior. Fasts and relentless workouts kept my weight around 190 pounds. I went to every diet guru I could and tried weird foods, including drinking regurgitated cow liquid, supposedly a high-protein substitute for regular food. I tried hypnotism and every fad: the grapefruit diet, the leek diet, the Atkins diet. Weight Watchers worked for me, but I wanted the silver bullet of weight loss, the easier, softer way to lose weight faster. It's the equivalent of the alcoholic switching from hard liquor to beer or wine. That's not the answer. An alcoholic still inevitably gets drunk.

No wonder sensible eating didn't work. When I binged, which was often, it looked like this: on the road visiting SSG stations, my dinner was the biggest shake Dairy Queen served (ten inches high) and two hot dogs. I supplemented that meal with sweets from our stations and endless packs of sugary gum and carbs until I was tired enough to go to bed. I hid it all. Living alone made it easy.

I'M YOUR KNIGHT

I met Syble Luckey on St. Patrick's Day in 1977 at Gallivan's, the decades-old downtown St. Paul headquarters for Irish revelry. Syble was a homemaker who had just ended an unhappy marriage. Syble's neighbor took her out on St. Patrick's Day to cheer her up. I was drinking with my old buddy John O'Malley and a friend from the oil business.

Syble was petite and pretty, a native of Alabama who married a hot shot Air Force jet pilot stationed in Pensacola, Florida. He served in Vietnam and joined Northwest Airlines after his discharge. Syble moved with him to Apple Valley, a sprawling middle-class suburb south of St. Paul. They had two children, Judd and Stephanie, ages eight and eleven. Syble ended up with very little alimony or child support.

She shared the details of her divorce with me that afternoon and evening at Gallivan's, and I delivered my alcohol-infused snow job: "Now that you've met me," I declared, "you don't have to worry about anything. I'll take care of you. I'm your knight in shining armor." I put on the full court press, and it was especially convincing after lots of drinks. Syble was a classy lady and a little remote, so winning her was a challenge.

Only days after that, Syble and I started dating, and very soon we were a couple. I continued my gambling junkets, only now I had a partner. We traveled to Las Vegas and Monte Carlo and got along famously. I remember bringing back $11,000 in winnings on one trip. All in francs. I was only allowed $10,000, so I gave Syble more than half the loot to carry and we sweated it as the customs official painstakingly, but not accurately, counted the francs.

We had great fun traveling, dining at the Twin Cities' most fashionable restaurants, and taking our children on outings. When I drank too much at the gaming table, she settled up and got me to our room. When I woke up with a horrendous hangover, she gave me cold packs and aspirin. When I ate too much, she passed it off as vacation largesse. Syble came by codependency naturally, having grown up with an alcoholic father and an addict brother. She neither drank too much nor overate, and yet our relationship revolved around food and alcohol. Her focus was her children and me. She started attending nursing school so she could support her kids. I helped with tuition and daily household expenses.

My word was good. I was her knight. Also codependent, I took care of Syble and her children. We became a family.

Looking back, I realize that in every encounter with a desirable woman, I "steamrolled" her. I came on strong. I was a gentleman; I wasn't a boor, but I took over. I didn't have relationships; I took hostages.

Having Syble in my life made me feel worthy. Here was a respectable, suburban homemaker who was becoming a nurse. Here was someone I could introduce to my kids and friends. Here was a woman of quality who really liked me. Maybe this time, the pairing would have a happy ending.

GETTING REAL

Just four months after I turned forty, in December 1978, Syble told me she was carrying my child. How did I feel? Like stepping on a rake. Abortion was out of the question for us, but I didn't feel ready to commit. Syble wanted marriage, and the pressure mounted over the spring and summer. That August, I went to the Northwest Territories to fish with my Decathlon friends.

I was a total novice on that trip. They told me to bring a snowmobile suit and a beekeeper's hat. No joke. The trip involved a jet and two float planes carrying us far into the wilderness. We wound up on a sand spit where lake trout were plentiful and clouds of black flies could take down a caribou. It was a world apart: flannel shirts and protective hats by day, dressing for dinner at night.

I had time to think and talk to my friends about this next step with Syble. I went home willing to say yes.

We told our four children about our impending marriage and about the baby. They were shocked and hurt that we kept the secret for months. Syble and I married on September 15, 1979, in a small ceremony in Reno. My sister Gail and her husband Don were our witnesses. I was so insensitive that I produced a ring three sizes too small for Syble. We had a celebration dinner, and I allowed myself two glasses of champagne. I figured that "controlled drinking" was a viable option (a slippery slope for anyone with the addictive gene).

Our beautiful daughter Anne Marie was born on December 26. Syble had a caesarian section, and our moms and I paced nervously in the waiting room at Fairview Southdale Hospital. Finally, the doctor appeared, peeled his mask off and grinned. "She's fine," he said.

SHE? I thought. *Did he mean Syble? By God, we were expecting a boy!*

Five minutes later, the nurse brought Anne Marie out to me and I held her for the first time. I fell in love again, just as I had when I first saw Jennie and John. We brought Anne Marie home to our newly remodeled, five-bedroom house in Hudson, Wisconsin. Only a few years later, when my love of water turned from houseboats to sailing, I named my first sailboat *Anne Marie*. Two more *Anne Marie* sailboats followed, each more beautiful than the one before. Just like my daughter.

Syble and I performed a codependent dance in our marriage. As I spent time with my male friends, she yearned for closeness between us and craved security and safety. But when Syble got "clingy," I pulled further away. She scared me. *Was she taking over my life? Trying to turn me into someone I wasn't?* Even though I was married, I never gave up my condo at Connemara. It was my safety net. My cocoon.

When Syble was confident and felt more secure, I moved closer. But cycling in the other direction, she sometimes expressed herself with ultimatums or verbal abuse. I ran to the safety of Connemara. And food.

We went to therapists. We tried to find equilibrium in our relationship. Mostly it was incendiary, not intimate. Codependents try to control other people, believing that they can change another person's behavior. Addicts try to control everything around them. No wonder we struggled to marital exhaustion.

MILK AND STUFF

By the time Syble and I married, SSG had transformed from gas stations to convenience stores, from selling cigarettes, snacks, and sodas to stocking groceries in a "mini store," filling two hundred square feet in our trial-run operation in Scanlon, Minnesota. When it had opened in 1976, Scanlon was the forerunner to Auto Stop's modern convenience stores.

The trigger for this strategic shift was prompted by Ma and Pa Clock. We had hired non-retired operators to run our stations in Tomahawk and Merrill, Wisconsin, who didn't like the part-time work and pay arrangement we set up for our senior operators. They decided to challenge it. They were the ones who said our clock system was a scam, a way to circumvent minimum wage rules. They even picketed their own stores. We had a right to fire them, and we did. That's just what they wanted. They slapped us with a lawsuit.

The issue went to court in Wisconsin, and my biggest fear was that others working for us might join a class action against us. That could have put SSG out of business. It didn't happen. The courts ruled against us, but the responsibility was shared. They gave us a $5,000 fine and ordered the plaintiffs to pay *our* lawyer's fees. We lost the case, but we won the battle.

That was the end of our "ma and pa" senior operators. We weren't going to take another chance. That's how we came up with our new concept—the combined gas station and convenience store. We had a shorthand phrase for the strategy: we called it "milk and stuff." Every Monday when the SSG staff met to review the previous week's performance, I asked about sales of "milk and stuff." The phrase became part of our corporate jargon, so we named Scanlon's new grocery section exactly that, "Milk and Stuff."

In 1971, our revenues came only from selling gasoline. Sales of cigarettes, snacks, and soda grew to five percent by 1975. But by the end of the 1970s, "milk and stuff" generated a respectable fifteen percent of our annual sales. We were onto something!

We spent the final years of the seventies converting our stations to convenience stores, and we used our own tractor-trailer units to ensure a steady supply of gasoline to more than thirty enlarged and remodeled stores. SSG's logo was popping up all over. In Wisconsin, we had new locations in New Richmond, Park Falls, Minoqua, Waupaca, Menomonie, Black River Falls, Ashland, Cumberland, New London, Whitehall, and Minong. In Minnesota, we opened new stations in Duluth and Scanlon.

Business was great, and we deserved our own headquarters. In 1978, we moved SSG's corporate offices from a second-story leased space on Second Street in downtown Hudson to new quarters on Coulee Road overlooking the St. Croix River. Formerly a Texaco gas station, we remodeled and doubled the building's size. We created the office I had envisioned years before: plush and professional with chrome and glass fixtures, leather couches, and a fireplace. Walls were painted in designer colors. Our corporate receptionist was positioned at a cool, glass "cashier's window." SSG's "executive row" shared the building with a real, functioning Auto Stop at street level. For Darcy Hield, the SSG headquarters was her first, big interior design project. She had joined Kathy Young's firm, and she amazed me with her creativity. (Darcy has tackled every one of my commercial and residential projects ever since, and I always say she makes us look better.)

On weekends and during the summers, Jennie and John spent time with me at our headquarters. I'll never forget the day my eight-year-old John watched our cashier open a small, round safe in the floor and pull out an impressive stack of bills to make change for SSG customers at the pump. John looked at the hole in the floor with amazement and announced with certainty, "Oh, so that's where money comes from!" (He still believes it comes from a hole in the floor.)

More than 250 people from Hudson celebrated our SSG office open house. I basked in the attention and excitement. And I drank too much. "Controlled drinking" wasn't working for me.

BOXED IN

My "boxes" were bumping into each other. I was finding it harder to keep them separate, and I knew I had to. No one could know the full extent of my binging on food and alcohol. But some of my friends and family were getting glimpses, no matter how hard I tried to cover up. I looked good, but I sure didn't feel good.

I asked my friend Neil from the Decathlon to have lunch with me. I noticed that he didn't drink. Some of my friends at the club didn't either. I was curious about that. Neil was in recovery from alcoholism, and he was board chair of St. Mary's treatment center in Minneapolis where Sharon got her help.

We sat in a booth at the Decathlon, and I laid it out: "I know you don't drink, and some of the others don't. I think alcohol is affecting my life. What do you think I should do about it?"

Neil said he couldn't judge whether I was alcoholic or not, but he suggested I talk to an experienced professional, George Mann, one of the godfathers of modern addiction treatment in Minnesota. George suggested that I try not drinking and he and I would meet regularly during that time.

Not long after that talk with George, I was hanging out in the bar at the Decathlon with my Diet Coke. A woman came into the bar—an unusual occurrence. We were mostly men in that dark-wood and red-leather hangout, and the guys started buying her drinks. After a while, the other guys left and it was just the two of us. I invited her to join me at the Thunderbird, a hotel and bar a couple blocks away.

Sitting at the Thunderbird bar, I was anxious, unsure of what to say or do. She drank wine, and I had my Diet Coke. Before long I switched to wine. With each drink, the anxiety melted away and I became Mr. Cool again. I used alcohol to drown my anxiety and quiet my nerves. A couple glasses worked like magic, and I was again in control.

When I told George Mann about it, he suggested the obvious: instead of taking that first drink, why not try admitting you're a little anxious? If you do, you'll feel better and you might not need the drink. Worth a shot.

I thought hard about that incident when I ran my five-miler the next day. I didn't want anything controlling my life. I committed to not drinking and being more honest about how I felt. I never used alcohol after that. For twenty-eight years, one day at a time, I've been free of alcohol.

Of course, that bold declaration never applied to binging on food.

Food was my primary addiction. I could let go of nicotine, speed, alcohol, and gambling, but only because I still had my most powerful drug: food. For most of us addicts, there is one, primary addiction that we seek above all others. If that drug is taken away from us, we'll settle for seconds, but only then.

OUT OF THE MOUTHS OF BABES

About the same time I confronted alcohol in my life, SSG landed in court, thanks to a gang of inquisitive school children. With all the news about gas shortages through the 1970s, teachers incorporated this topic and its implications into their classes. In a tiny town called

Park Falls, Wisconsin, a grade school teacher asked her class to study how gas stations set their prices. She told them to visit the gas station operators in their town and interview them. The kids talked to the guy running the local Clark station and asked him how he set his price. "Well," he said, "I talk to Joe at Holiday."

The Holiday guy said, "I talk to Ken at Auto Stop."

This is how the petroleum industry operated for decades, and this was all we knew.

When the teacher shared her report with the Wisconsin attorney general, the state decided to make SSG an example. They charged Auto Stop with "predatory pricing"—another term for price-fixing. We never denied it.

Our operations director, my brother-in-law Don, was shocked. People in our business did this every day. Other industries did, too. Do you think it's a coincidence that McDonald's and Burger King change their prices about the same time? Is it an accident that banks pick the same interest rates? SSG entered a "no contest" plea; Don was charged with a felony and fined $25,000. SSG was fined the same amount. Of course, I knew about the practices in my industry. We were no different than anyone else. But because Don was responsible for SSG operations, the onus fell on him. It was a painful, strained time for Don, my sister Gail, and me. Don was convicted of a felony and, ultimately, the governor of Wisconsin pardoned him.

Don wanted out of the business. About the same time, our accountant advised me to invest SSG's considerable operating earnings into new ventures so we could avoid paying excess earnings taxes. "Why not buy Wisconsin farmland," our guy from Arthur Andersen suggested? "You know that's going to increase in value."

So we bought Croixland Farms, two farms with registered

Holsteins worth $10,000 to $20,000 each. Cows that dined on special hay shipped from Colorado (the same hay the Queen of England gave her horses). We got into breeding high-class cows, flying them to Grand Ole Opry, and showing them on the stage where they were auctioned off. We also had sixty head of dairy cattle. They lived so well they gave milk three times a day!

When the State of Wisconsin held its annual "Farm City Day" celebration, we transported special visitors to Croixland Farms in limousines so they could tour our hygienic barns, witness modern milking, and soak up the sights and smells of rural Wisconsin.

My brother-in-law Don ran Croixland Farms for me. Though both of us were intrigued by the "designer livestock" scene, we never made any money on the venture.

But investing in real estate was different. I had a knack for picking good locations when I chose sites for SSG stations; and I used that skill to select my first, of many, real estate investments.

I teamed up with two respected companies in Hudson, Keller Construction and Elliot Anderson Architects, to build a large office building on spec at the corner of Highway 36 and McKnight Road in Maplewood, a growing St. Paul suburb. We were only halfway through construction when the executive director of a local hospital approached me. He represented a group of doctors who worked with his hospital, and he proposed turning the whole building into a clinic. That relationship lasted for twenty years.

EXTREME MAKEOVER

My business life in Hudson, the expansion of SSG, and my new ventures, including Croixland Farms and the Maplewood Clinic, put me in the papers more often. By this time, I'd replaced the high I got from alcohol with multiple, exciting new projects and deals. I was an "activity addict," and these new ventures gave me a huge rush.

Looking back, my addictions actually gave me an edge in business, for a while. I truly believed in my "terminal uniqueness." I believed I had the guts, the smarts, and the gumption to accomplish anything. My addictions fueled that. And, when I needed energy and stamina, sugar and carbs kept me going. Longer, faster, better than anything else. I believed I needed my "drugs" to keep me in the game. Ultimately, those drugs turned on me. It was years before I realized that my drug-altered mind led me to some ill-advised decisions.

The owner of the Milwaukee Bucks basketball team asked me to join him in pursuing a franchise for cable TV in western Wisconsin when the industry was just getting started. I invested heavily in St. Croix Cablevision, but we didn't win the franchise. Still, it was exciting and I noticed the familiar rush it gave me.

I enjoyed all the positive recognition of my ventures, even when they didn't always pan out. I was becoming a community leader, and I wanted to do something meaningful for Hudson's aging downtown area. It bothered me that Stillwater, our neighbor on the Minnesota side of the St. Croix River, enjoyed more tourism, shopping, and popularity. We were like the ugly, stepsister. If Hudson had an extreme makeover, we just might catch up to Stillwater.

In 1980, I decided to buy two buildings on Main Street that had once housed the Ben Franklin, a hardware store, and—in the 1880s—an opera house. I set about transforming these vacant and dilapidated old buildings into a home for small, specialty retail shops and offices.

After many trips to the state historical society in Madison, conferring on plans and architectural designs, I got the entire block listed on the National Register of Historic Buildings. I renamed the buildings The Opera House and 2nd Street Crossing.

When we tore out the innards of those buildings, I waded through the debris and found memorabilia from their earliest days. We used some of the original stone, wood, glass, and pieces of metal ceilings in our remodeling plan.

By the end of the decade, we had plenty of first-class tenants, including antique, furniture, crafts, and frame stores, a bookseller, a gift shop, and an ice cream parlor and toy store. The Hudson Area Chamber of Commerce set up shop there and so did the Hudson Senior Citizen Center.

As all of this was happening, I had an image in my mind's eye: why not create a restaurant in the building's basement? Make it reminiscent of the Opera House's earlier days. Call it Act 2 at the Opera House? Turning that vision into reality was no easy plan. I supervised the work crew that hand-carried four feet of dirt out of that basement in buckets so we had enough headroom for the restaurant. As we cleared the basement, we found more metal ceilings with large beams. It was like being on an archeological dig and finding the ancient aqueducts of Constantinople.

We created a beautiful jazz club, about 2,500 square feet, seating about sixty to a hundred people. The space was a classy blend of new and old: stone walls, old wood beams, and a modern bar. Visitors entering Act 2 passed a railing from the balcony of the original Opera House and looked through original stained glass that was incorporated into the new décor. We built a stage with curtains so we could have live performers, as well as a screen for movie nights.

I designed everything in that jazz club and restaurant down to the menu and the dress of the wait staff. Randy Penner, a successful,

Hudson-based watercolorist who doubled as my one-man art department, guided me in all things visual. Randy had a sophisticated eye, and he designed the logos for every one of my business ventures, as well as every boat I owned. I commissioned Randy to create a special watercolor for a prominent spot in Act 2.

Though I was a perfectionist about virtually every detail of Act 2, I overlooked the basics of food service. We planned a "dress rehearsal" opening of Act 2 over lunch, serving forty of our SSG employees. Two, excruciating hours passed before our inedible lunch of burgers and salads arrived. I turned my obsessive mind to the kitchen.

When we officially opened on May 21, 1981, the setting and service was perfection. Our guests raved, and Act 2 attracted a steady stream of repeat customers who loved Al Tedesco, our house singer. Al owned a couple radio stations in the Midwest, and he was quite the man-about-town. Larger than life, like my old pal John O'Malley.

We staged Marx Brothers movie nights with a special menu (Groucho and Harpo Burgers) and a special fish-and-chips night in honor of Princess Di's wedding. On the kids' menu, my youngest daughter, Anne Marie, inspired the Anna Banana sandwich.

We kept the fun rolling with new attractions. One of our waiters sang medleys from the Broadway hit, *Fiddler on the Roof*, and the reigning Miss Minnesota played our grand piano.

I loved all the hoopla, attention, and excitement of launching Act 2, but the day-to-day reality wasn't satisfying. I'd walk in and always notice what was wrong, what needed to be fixed. I couldn't relax and enjoy the outcome. The perfectionist in me didn't allow it.

Even so, the community of Hudson loved my contributions to Main Street and the *Hudson Star-Observer* was particularly laudatory. In one column, reporter Steve Johnson wrote, "It isn't often that the character of a whole town changes in a single day. Hudson has turned the corner."

I was hooked on the excitement of that project and, frankly, the shameless adulation.

About the same time, the owner and publisher of the *Hudson Star-Observer* approached me about buying the newspaper and becoming its publisher. Two of the owners of Hudson State Bank also asked me to consider buying their interests and those of their other three partners.

I was flattered by the overtures, but I declined both. The entrepreneur in me could see the potential of growing that venerable little newspaper and putting my money into a thriving bank with a loyal customer base. But the addict in me couldn't take the chance. I regretted that decision for years.

Here's what held me back. These two ventures employed lots of people, required intense management attention, and demanded interaction with the public and independent boards of directors. *What if I was found out? What if people knew who I really was? What if they knew about the crazy relationship I had with food? What if they got a glimpse of the shame, guilt, and depression I hid deep inside? What if the "box" that contained my carefully orchestrated role as a successful Hudson businessman became tainted with that other "box"—my addiction? What if people discovered how self-centered, sick, and sneaky I could be when my drugs were at stake?* I was already walking a tightrope with my own company, SSG. These new ventures could trigger a very public fall.

I had to keep a lid on that box.

FIVE

I'LL KEEP EATING UNTIL I'M SICK

BARING THE HOLE IN MY SOUL

What am I doing here? I'm scared. I don't know what to say. What if I break down in front of these strangers? Maybe I'll take a pass when my turn comes to talk. Nobody can force me to bare my sorry soul.

I was seated in a circle of about twenty-five uneasy people like me at a Parkview Hospital retreat center in Minneapolis. My wife, Syble, had just dropped me off with my duffle bag and wished me luck.

Every one of us in the circle was compulsive about something. Alcohol, cigarettes, gambling, sex, prescription drugs, shopping, work. For me it was food.

Someone else started.

"I'm here because I can't stay away from the casinos. My marriage is breaking up over this. I'm drowning in debt. I'm scared."

Then another person.

"I work all the time because it makes me feel good and people think I'm a hero. I know I hide out at work. I'm exhausted, and I don't have any friends left."

And another.

"I drink when I'm sad or frustrated. I drink when I'm happy. I drink when I'm alone to feel less lonely. I drink when I'm around people to feel like I fit in. I plan my days around drinking. I'm sick and tired of it."

And another.

"I eat. I binge and I hide it. I go to different grocery stores so they don't see me buying ice cream and sweets too often. I rarely see my friends anymore. I can't do the things I once loved because of my weight. I just go home after work and eat in front of the TV. In the morning, I feel ashamed, depressed, and hungover from all the sugar."

Then it was my turn. The moment of truth.

"I've been eating to feel better since I was a kid. I'm out of control. I binge in private and take laxatives. I work out like a madman and fast for days to make up for my binges and maintain my weight. I've had one failed marriage, and I'm in another one that's failing. How I eat has something to do with my relationships, but I don't understand what it is. I'm here because food is affecting my life. I'm forty-four. I can't live like this."

Okay. I said it. People didn't gasp. The floor didn't part and pull me into some black abyss.

The more people talked, the more I felt like I belonged there. Others in this circle struggled like I did. Nobody was passing judgment. *They get me. I get them.*

It feels safe…like I'm home.

TEETERING ON THE TIGHT ROPE

With no alcohol, nicotine, or speed in my system, it was clear that food altered my mood dramatically. I used it to pull out of my blues. I used it to come down from my highs. I used it to manage my anxiety. And it worked for a short time. In the beginning of a food binge, I was highly creative and I could put together deals in twenty-four hours that typically took weeks. But maintaining that perfect state of mind I called "normal" was a tightrope walk. I lost my balance all the time.

Living with others, I had to be careful. I'd eat a bowl of ice cream, then wait until everyone else was in bed and finish off the whole half-gallon. I didn't want to get caught. Then I had to replace whatever I ate so that no one noticed. I went out to lunch with business associates, and if somebody said the cheesecake was great, I'd order the whole cake for the table.

Syble and I would have a wonderful, five-course dinner at some fancy restaurant, and I went back to my condo alone and ate a jar of peanuts and a whole bag of pretzels or trail mix.

That's another reason I kept my separate place at Connemara after I got married. I could do what I wanted, eat what I wanted, when I wanted.

But it was getting harder to live with myself. I was a faker. I went to Weight Watchers and learned about healthy eating and talked "the talk." I honestly believed it. I bought sugar-free ice cream and baked chips for the kids when they visited. I stocked pre-made, healthy meals and soups from the best grocery stores, but I ate the whole box of saltines that went with the soup! I worked out at the Decathlon Club like some health freak, but my prime motive wasn't muscle tone, it was burning calories after binging. My good friends at the club didn't know this about me. Because I maintained a decent weight—and I didn't binge around them—they thought I was a normal guy.

Syble and her mom were both terrific Southern cooks, and I loved their meals. I was disciplined at the table and ate normal quantities. But then I found a way to cut out and binge in private.

I was feeling more ashamed about how I used food. When I finally decided to ban foods at home that tempted me, that tactic failed, too. If all I had was dry, shredded wheat, I ate the whole box. I might be depressed, tired, even elated—it didn't matter—I wanted something in my mouth. Something going down. Something to soothe. Something to comfort and relax me.

The carbs and sugar always relieved the pressure inside.

I was embarrassed by the laxatives. I used them often enough that it was unhealthy. I was walking a fine line, and I went right to the edge of getting sick.

When I tried fad diets—all eggs, all grapefruit, cow protein, Atkins—I lost weight and felt in control for a few weeks, sometimes even a month. I inevitably went back to my old ways—gaining weight, despite heavy workouts.

I resorted to total fasting for up to two weeks at a time. No food, just water, adding juices on the ninth day. I felt my best when I was fasting; I felt total control. I was creative and energized with projects. I saw immediate results.

Here's the catch. I had a smaller belt size and got a lot accomplished in my business, but I still had the same problems and desperate feelings. My secret life was closing in on me. If I got too much sugar or too many carbs, I sunk into despair; or I became the opposite—manic and compulsive. I knew that if I went out for lunch and had a piece of apple pie, I had to maintain that same sugar level all day until I went to sleep—or crashed. I kept thinking, "If I can just stay at this level, I'll be perfect."

If I crashed, I felt physically and emotionally sick. So I started eating to restore my equilibrium. I felt like I was trying to manage a crazy person I didn't understand.

Food had power over me, more than I wanted to admit. I was like the alcoholic who couldn't resist picking up that first drink. Only for me, it was trail mix or chips. The struggle was not about willpower; it was about *being powerless*. I'd keep eating until I got sick. If my supply were endless, I honestly didn't know when, or if, I'd stop eating. Alcoholics said the same thing about drinking. That's what scared me.

MY UNHOLY ALLIANCE

For nearly ten years, almost every week, I'd been seeing a personal therapist. I was trying to understand my rocky relationship with Syble and my part in it. I was involved in a small support group of three others grappling with their failed marriages, and we were becoming close friends. I had some solid breakthroughs, but I thought there was more going on than Syble and me. *What about the food?*

My therapist continued to focus on the marriage, and I insisted it also had *something* to do with food. *Do I eat because I'm in a bad relationship, or is my relationship bad because of my unholy alliance with food? Is it both?* I turned this over in my head. I was more honest with my therapist about my eating than I'd ever been.

She finally agreed to refer me to a therapist with experience in eating disorders. I sat down with the new therapist, Ann, and told her the whole, sick story. Sneaking sweets as a kid and stealing money to buy more, chasing sleazy doctors for diet pills in my twenties, count-less binges and mounting shame, dangerous fad diets and fasts in my thirties, secret promises to change, repeated failures, growing hope-lessness, and a life scarred by lies, secrets, and manipulation.

Ann listened and offered me a lifeline: "Burt," she said, "I believe you."

I was, at first, stunned. Then I felt outright relief, and the tears came. My struggle was not imaginary. It was not simply about self-control. This was the first time someone really understood me. Ann offered me real hope for the first time in my life.

"It's called a compulsivity clinic," she said. "You'll spend four days there in your *early discovery* period. You'll learn about compulsive overeating and addiction. It's a disease, Burt, not a moral failing. It's not about personal weakness. You'll learn about the 12-Step program, and you'll begin to acquire tools that will help you live without your addiction having the upper hand. You'll never be free of your addic-tion, but you'll learn to be healthy and happy in spite of it. This may seem impossible to you, now; but someday you may even be grateful for this sickness.

"You'll be given an 'aftercare' plan," she told me, "and that's when you'll start your recovery with food choices and temptations around you all the time. Recovery is hard work. It requires a lot of personal honesty and commitment, but you've done the hardest work. You've struggled alone.... Are you willing?"

"I'll try anything. My whole life, I've been willing to do what was necessary to feel normal."

Here's the irony. This was in May 1982. The very same year I said "yes" to this lifeline, the leaders of Hudson, Wisconsin, congratulated me for "changing the face of downtown Hudson forever." Here I was, setting in motion a personal journey that was about to change the face of my whole *life* forever.

BOOT CAMP OF THE HEART AND MIND

My four days at the compulsivity clinic were intense: boot camp for the heart and mind; small group sessions, chalk talks, and evening meetings with speakers; sleeping in bunk beds with a bunch of guys in the same, big room (when I was accustomed to luxury suites in the MGM Grand). It was like a twenty-eight-day treatment for alcoholism and drug abuse—only compressed into four, long, emotional days. Before I got to the clinic, I had wished I was a simple, garden-variety alcoholic and could qualify for the "luxury" of a full twenty-eight-day experience.

When I decided to get help, Overeaters Anonymous (OA)—a 12-Step program patterned after Alcoholics Anonymous—was still a small movement. In 1980 President Jimmy Carter congratulated OA on its twentieth anniversary. He declared that obesity had become a major, public health problem with a "startling" thirty-five percent of American adults considered obese, costing the U.S. $147 billion a year. In 2009, the Centers for Disease Control said that sixty-six percent of American adults were overweight or obese. On top of that, more than fifty percent of us didn't get enough physical activity. Is it any wonder that our children and grandchildren are following the same dangerous patterns in epidemic numbers?

During those four days at the clinic, I learned about my addiction to food. I was surprised to learn that food can be more addictive than tobacco, drugs, alcohol, or gambling, and just as destructive. Here's why: we can't live without food. Each time a food addict like me eats,

I'm in danger of succumbing to my compulsion. It's one thing to give up alcohol and ban liquor from my home, but I can't live without food. I have to *live with the enemy.*

In this society, food is everywhere and there is no stigma attached to eating—unless you're already fat. Anna Wintour, the editor of *Vogue*, traveled to Minnesota in 2009 and "kindly" (her word) described most of the people she saw as "little houses."

We associate good food with good times and celebration. Many of us reward ourselves with food, especially sweets, "because we deserve it." In 2009, the average American consumed twenty-two teaspoons of sugar a day. That's twenty percent more than in 1970. Our hosts encourage us to have second helpings, and we often oblige in order to be appreciative guests. In some families food and love are synonymous. That's how it was in my Ellsworth, Wisconsin, farm family.

We are hesitant to bring up issues of weight, even with people we love. Surprisingly, an alcohol or drug intervention seems easier. Even doctors dodge the weight issue. I was struck by a commentary by Dr. Jeremy Brown, an associate professor of emergency medicine at George Washington University Hospital. In a May 2008 editorial in the *Washington Post*, Brown said, "I have been doing the unthinkable, and the word is out. I am an emergency physician in Washington, and I've started talking to my patients about their weight. It has taken me a while to pluck up the courage…. For 15 years, I have broached virtually every delicate subject—from sexual histories to the cough that is really cancer—in the noisy, impersonal setting of a busy ER. It is expected of me. It is my job. So why has it been so hard to talk about this? With an epidemic of obesity in the United States, why are so many doctors skittish about discussing obesity with its sufferers? The truth is, I don't know."

Dr. Brown asserted that young docs need to learn in medical school how to talk about obesity. Lay people don't know what to say either. We have no training.

But consider this. When I was in the depths of my addiction, I looked healthy. Because I resorted to fasting and frenetic exercise, I wasn't overweight. Compulsive overeating can be a hidden disease. An overeater may only be a pound overweight, or even underweight and suffering from anorexia nervosa. This illness has little to do with weight. The real problem is this: compulsive overeaters can't control their food intake on their own.

ADMITTING I'M POWERLESS

In those four days at the clinic, I faced how irrational and self-destructive compulsive overeating can be. People like me have done things that it's hard to imagine any sane person doing. We've driven miles in the dead of night to satisfy a food craving. We've eaten food that was frozen, burnt, stale, or even dangerously spoiled. We've eaten off other people's plates, off the floor, off the ground. We've even eaten food we've dug out of garbage cans.

When I overeat, I know I'm harming my body. When I was stoned on sugar, I made poor business decisions. I couldn't maintain my "high" from food, so I sunk into depression. There were times when I couldn't focus long enough to plan a business meeting. I isolated myself so I could hang out with my favorite companions: my binge foods. My business got half my attention; my relationships with my wife and children suffered. At family functions I couldn't be present in the way I wanted. I was focused on food, not people. That's when I hit my "bottom," the place where I decided life was no longer worth living.

When that happens, an addict chooses life or death. I never considered suicide, as some addicts do, but I was committing a slow suicide, *just as my father had.*

I was ready for Step One of the 12 Steps of Overeaters Anonymous: "We admitted we were powerless over food—that our lives had become unmanageable."

For a control freak like me, admitting I'm powerless over *anything* is unimaginable. But I was beat in May 1982. The clinic helped me see that my food addiction is an affliction of body, mind, and spirit.

Today, we know that obesity and lack of exercise is linked to coronary heart disease, stroke, high blood pressure, Type 2 diabetes, colon and breast cancer, and depression. According to the U.S. Office of Health and Human Services, these chronic diseases affect a hundred million Americans, cause seven out of every ten deaths, and eat up two out of every three dollars we spend on health care. Among obese women, there's a significant increase in uterine cancer, gallbladder disease, and gallstones. Even the babies of obese mothers suffer twice the infant mortality rate.

Here's the heartbreaking statistic cited by Dr. Peter G. Lindner, past president of the American Society of Bariatric Physicians: less than five percent of dieters maintain their weight loss for at least five years (*Overeaters Anonymous,* 1980). People like me know that we can't control our food compulsion on any lasting basis. We have proof; we've spent our lives trying and failing. Our performance is not a question of willpower. Most compulsive overeaters have exceptional willpower. How else could I fast on water and fruit juice for two weeks?

Physicians agree that compulsive overeating is an illness that can't be controlled by willpower. It's a chronic illness like diabetes or heart disease. I'm not like normal people when it comes to eating; I never will be. When a normal person gets full, s/he loses interest in eating more food. When I overindulge, I crave more and can't quit. I didn't choose to have this illness, and I can't choose to be free of it. But I *can* live a healthy life even though the illness is my constant companion.

And because I am an addict, I am prone to picking up my other addictions again, if I can't satisfy my cravings with food. It's called "cross addiction."

I'm not a bad person; I'm a sick person. As I learned more about my disease, I realized that I could give up blaming myself and sinking into guilt and shame—the morass that kept me stuck and over-whelmed for decades.

DECONSTRUCTING DENIAL

I had to give up my illusion of control, admit my powerlessness, and own up to my unmanageable life. That's a tall order for a guy who looks good, owns a successful business, and travels through life with the illusion of confidence. I had the "look good" down pat, but I flunked the "feel good" part of life's equation.

Here is where the mind and spirit come in. I have a mental obses-sion with food. As a youngster, I learned to push down my problems with food; it worked for years. Then the very thing that seemed to be my "friend" turned on me. Over time, I lost my ability to say no. My friend became my enemy. No amount of self-control or weight loss mattered. The day always came when too much food looked irresist-ible, no matter how firm my resolutions. Sooner or later, I started overeating until the cycle got worse and I was out of control. Again.

By the time I arrived at the compulsivity clinic, my denial of this disease had mostly evaporated. Even so, my assignment was a Step

One inventory designed to put my powerlessness and unmanageability into concrete terms, describe my patterns of compulsive overeating from my earliest days. I had to write down how it felt, what I did to get food, how I compensated for the high-caloric intake. I had to be specific about how unmanageable my life had become and include every painful detail I could name: the failed marriages, poor business decisions, being less of a dad; trying to control every detail of my life and other people's lives; chronic sadness hidden behind false cheer, my feelings numbed, and the growing hole in my soul.

I read my story out loud to the group. This wasn't a striptease; it was the "full monty" of personal disclosure.

Like everyone else in the group, I resorted to "victim thinking." If other people would just do their part, keep their promises, appreciate my efforts, and do things my way, life would be better and I wouldn't be driven to food, *right?* A page from Step One of the Overeaters Anonymous book hit me between the eyes:

"we didn't realize how much we had damaged ourselves and others by attempting to manage every detail of life. It was only after we began to recover that we saw the childish self-centered-ness of our willful actions. By trying to control others through manipulation and direct force, we had hurt our loved ones. When we tried to control ourselves, we wound up demoralized. Even when we succeeded, it wasn't enough to make us happy. We hid from our pain by eating, so we didn't learn from our mistakes; we never grew up."

Ouch.

But here's the amazing thing: when I could admit my powerless-ness over food and surrender, the door opened to a new-found power.

For the first time in my life I recognized, acknowledged, and accepted the truth about myself. I was a compulsive overeater; I had a disease, and there was a solution. But I had to surrender first. I had to let go of my old beliefs about control and tackling my problems alone. I had to ask for help and believe in a power that was greater than myself. The understanding of that power is left to each one of us. Newcomers to recovery are simply asked to be open-minded. In time, even atheists and agnostics arrive at their own definitions. For me, that power is God.

DISCOVERING 'THE GOLDEN THREAD'

Overeaters Anonymous was active in 1982 when I got into recovery, but there were far fewer meetings than we see today. My "aftercare" assignment from the compulsivity clinic was going to OA. I picked a meeting in Minneapolis and—like at Weight Watchers—I walked into a room full of women. They greeted me warmly, and I joined the circle of others perched on folding chairs. Just like the clinic, they talked openly about their overeating. They even laughed about the more bizarre episodes. They were just like me. There's a golden thread that is woven through all of us in this program. We share the same disease, and it unites us.

I was inspired when some of the veteran members stood up, gave their names, and reported how much weight they had lost. Some shed as much as a hundred pounds, and most hadn't binged—or "slipped," as we call it—in months, even years.

I found a sponsor, and I met with Margie weekly. I called her if I found myself in a slippery place where I needed support. We "worked the Steps" by reading the OA "Big Book" together and discussing each of the 12 Steps and how they applied to me. At the meetings, I learned how to cope in a healthy way, especially when I was vulnerable. I learned helpful acronyms:

HALT stands for hungry, angry, lonely, tired. When I'm feeling any or all of these feelings, I'm in danger of an overeating slip. I have to be watchful and call my sponsor, go to a meeting, read the Big Book, or meditate and pray on my situation.

HOW stands for honest, open, and willing. If I can be all three most of the time, I can stay in healthy recovery. HOW means I won't lie to myself. I'll be receptive to help and support, and I'll be willing to use the tools I've been given. I do none of this perfectly, but I never stop trying to be honest, open, and willing in all aspects of my life. Not just how I eat.

My disease is cunning, baffling, powerful, and patient. I must never forget that. Even if I'm not overeating, it's still with me. It's a progressive disease that gets stronger with time, no matter what I do. While I'm attending my weekly OA meeting, my disease is out in the parking lot doing one-arm push-ups.

YOU GOTTA HAVE A PLAN

Overeaters Anonymous doesn't recommend diets. It offers support and the 12 Steps gives me the best "architecture for living" I've ever known. I worked with my sponsor and a dietician to come up with an eating plan I could live with: three, moderate, measured meals a day with nothing in between and an apple at bedtime; and no "binge" foods—alcohol, sugar, refined carbohydrates. These are the "exciting" foods that threaten my sobriety. For me, they are chips of any kind, trail mix, pretzels, popcorn, sugar-free fudgesicles, ice cream, and candy.

I call them exciting because I'm powerfully drawn to them. I gave up sugar after my first OA meeting. I also gave up red meat and pork.

Here's how compulsive I am: in my earlier Weight Watchers days, they recommended eating red meat only once a week. I concluded that giving up red meat forever—no exceptions—could only be better! I haven't eaten red meat in nearly forty years.

Some people in OA measure and weigh all their food at each meal. I didn't find that necessary, but I was always willing if I couldn't keep on track.

Abstinence from compulsive overeating is the most important thing in my life. I know that if I put recovery first, I can be the person I was meant to be—in my relationships, in my work, in my community.

Early on, I learned there is no such thing as perfection. I'm human, flawed and weak. When I have a slip in my 12-Step program, my first responsibility is to own up to it, learn from it, and make amends if I need to. A person in the program calls this "cleaning up my side of the street."

CHARGED WITH 'ROCKET FUEL'

The streets in my own business life were multiplying. I was fully engaged in the thrill of commercial development. I was only in recovery less than a year when I bought about ten acres of prime property on "Hudson Hill" in 1983—an area about one mile from Hudson's historic downtown district. The property was in foreclosure, and my brother Dennis helped me negotiate the deal with some of his friends at American National Bank. I subdivided the property, laid out a plan for roads, sewers, and utilities, and went to work finding tenants over the next two years: a restaurant, a fast food outlet, two motels, and an office building.

I felt like I was running on rocket fuel. People call it "the pink cloud" in early recovery. I wasn't overeating; I attended regular OA meetings; I continued my workouts, and I felt charged with new health and energy. I had stamina, focus, and enthusiasm for life. I was living life on life's terms, and when I hit the inevitable speed bumps, I turned to my sponsor, meetings, and the tools of OA, instead of food.

I felt great. Before recovery, I led a double life—the public persona of the responsible businessman, husband, and father and the private life of a compulsive overeater. It took inhuman energy to live two, parallel lives at once. Now I had only one life and I poured all I had into it.

Within five years of that first Hudson Hill venture, I created Southside Center, a 30,000-square-foot shopping center, also in the hill district. I anchored the shopping center with an Auto Stop gas station and a Mr. Movies store, a franchise I had recently acquired with my partner, Kevin Vance. I initially bought the land to beat out a gas station competitor, but the venture turned out to be an excellent investment property that paid the tuition for private schools for all my grandchildren. I realized I could "do good" by doing well.

The deals were coming fast, and I welcomed them. Honestly, they gave me the "high" I missed from overeating. I have an addict's temperament, and I was doing what addicts in recovery usually do. I simply substituted one addictive behavior for another. If I couldn't get high on carbs and sweets anymore, I could soar on dicey, challenging, often eleventh-hour deals that delivered a guaranteed adrenaline rush.

In 1983, although I knew virtually nothing about the sand and gravel business, my brother Dennis and I discussed the possibility of us buying Yellow River Supply, a large commercial sand and gravel operation based in Turtle Lake, Wisconsin. They had six ready-mix plants and sand and gravel operations in western Wisconsin communities. Construction was picking up after the early 1980's recession. Dennis had recently retired from American Hoist and Derrick, and was pursuing a business investment. Not only did Dennis negotiate the purchase in 1984, he managed it so well that it turned into a solid profit for seventeen years until we sold it in 2001. Dennis and I had 44.4% percent ownership in Yellow River and our brother Ron owned 11.2%. Ron continues to work with me today and is my financial and business advisor. During the time we owned Yellow River Supply, I only visited the Turtle Lake office once because Dennis was masterful in his management. He did not need me hovering.

PAINFUL CLARITY

Many marriages end once one partner gets into recovery. Sure, the drug, alcohol, or other compulsive behavior is gone, but the rules of engagement change, too. I had three years in the 12-Step program of Overeaters Anonymous when Syble and I divorced in February 1985. Though I was committed to Syble, I had repeated the dynamics of my first marriage. As long as I fed my addiction, I never had the courage to share my real self with anyone.

Even so, Syble and I could work side by side. She was a good sport when, not long after our divorce, I launched into another new deal: buying a Taco John's franchise to occupy a potential hot spot right in the expanding Hudson Hill. The location was a corner at 11th Street and Coulee Road where an A&W Root Beer once stood. Once again I wanted to ensure that a competing gas station and convenience store didn't move in, because my station was just down the street. What did I know about the fast-food business? I hired a manager, and she and Syble traveled to Taco John's headquarters in Cheyenne, Wyoming, for management training. In typical Burt-style, I handled the big picture for the venture, the design and look of the restaurant, including original art by Randy Penner. I always believed that it didn't cost much more to go first class.

When we opened in June 1986, it was a quiet affair. Even so, everybody in Hudson seemed to show up. Ours was the first fast-food franchise in town. Cars lined up around the block. We ran out of food four times in our first day, and the Taco John's honchos from Cheyenne said it was the biggest opening day in their company's history. Thankfully, Kevin and Rita Vance, Taco John's owners from nearby Menomonie, Wisconsin, stopped in the next day, and I recruited them to work at the steam table and teach us the ropes.

We were over our heads. Even with training, our manager and Sybil stumbled. They didn't know enough about scheduling help, properly ordering supplies, or tracking expenses. It just came at them too fast. But even with our inept practices, we had record-setting receipts.

The following Monday I asked Kevin to meet with me at SSG in downtown Hudson. I got right to the point. "Kevin," I said, "I've got too much going on to oversee my Taco John's, and you know we're not equipped to do it. I see two options. You buy me out or we become partners and you run the stores."

Twenty-four hours later, Kevin took the partner option. We agreed on a value for our stores and combined them into a company we called TJ Management. I owned fifty-one percent and Kevin ran the operations. We went on to build several more Taco John's restaurants and a number of Mr. Movies' video rental stores, and we acquired the Blimpy's franchise for the State of Wisconsin.

The Hudson Taco John's and the Hudson Mr. Movies both became number-one stores in their franchise groups nationally. I credit Kevin with those successes. He was our "operations guy" with a strong strategic business sense. He brought his intelligence, planning, attention to detail, and discipline to our enterprise. He was a gem of a partner.

MY SSG POSSE

The "highs" of these new deals kept me wanting more while my sister Gail and her staff ran SSG. Over the years, my kid sister had advanced from my kitchen table accountant right out of college to chief operating officer overseeing every key component of some forty SSG stores. She assembled a strong team around her and leaned heavily on her key people, especially Larry Mitchell and Sue Kenall Zappa. Gail is the soul of SSG. Every major decision I make, and even most minor ones, pass through Gail's "filter." She is my confidante, partner, and "Tonto." We talk almost daily, and we never have cross words. Whenever we don't agree, eventually I discover that she is right. She's a problem-solver and crisis manager, and she always remains true to her principles.

Larry Mitchell joined SSG as a young, college-educated go-getter in his twenties, willing to learn the business from the bottom up. He soon became a supervisor, traveling the circuit, overseeing our stores. He became vice president of operations, developed the convenience food side of our business, and contributed much to our company's growth over the twenty years he worked with us. He made our

Hudson Amoco station the number-one dealer-operated store in the U.S., and he created one of the top dealer-operated convenience stores in Woodbury, Minnesota.

Sue Zappa ran our top Amoco in Hudson, tackled many complex management responsibilities, and ultimately succeeded Larry as SSG's vice president of operations.

Gail, Larry, Sue, and the entire SSG staff gave me the freedom to pursue my new ventures, including an opportunity that landed in my lap with just twenty-four hours to act.

I was having lunch in 1988 with the owners of the State Bank of Hudson (my business bank). They told me about a prime piece of property in Woodbury, Minnesota, twenty-five acres slated to be Woodbury Town Center. The property was in foreclosure. Their bank held the first mortgage, and State Bank of Hudson was the bank of record in the foreclosure. This was long before Woodbury became the fastest-growing community in the U.S. The suburb was still a huge expanse of old farmsteads and modest housing developments just east of downtown St. Paul along the Interstate 94 corridor leading to the St. Croix River and Wisconsin.

Woodbury had promise. Real estate developers with good instincts knew it, but the country was in a real estate recession in the mid to late eighties. Still, Woodbury city planners already had a new city hall on the books right across the street from Town Center.

"If you want to buy it," the bankers assured me, "we'll finance it, but you've got to act fast. The foreclosure will be official tomorrow at five P.M."

Right after lunch, I went back to my Connemara condo and began putting the deal together. Working with a yellow legal pad, I began to assemble my team. I was in my manic mode. I dipped into handfuls of peanuts and raisins to fuel my work. No dinner, just protein and junk food. I call it a "slip" in my OA program. Had I not reached out to my sponsor for help, that evening might have exploded into a full "relapse" with days of accelerated compulsive overeating and only sickness and shame at the end of it.

I got my longtime attorney, Don Campbell, on the phone and asked him to contact the banks involved in the foreclosure transaction. We had to get contracts written and come up with the down payment of $2 million the next day. I worked all that night on the details, and I put in a call to my old friend Jim Emison. I described the deal and told Jim I wanted him to be my financial partner. "How much money do you need?" he asked simply.

"One million," I answered.

"Well," he said, "I'm leaving for Canada tomorrow morning, so call my secretary and tell her where to wire it. I'm in."

Then I called Scott Steindorf, the owner of the purchase agreement. He stood to lose about half-a-million dollars he'd already invested if the sale didn't close the next day. Scott, a twenty-something entrepreneur and big risk taker, had the right vision for that prime property, but he was about ten years too early. He imagined the best stores and shops, first-class construction, a magnet for all the new homeowners putting down roots in suburban Woodbury. Scott was a wonderful salesman and a polished con, but he didn't have the "patient money" to make the deal work and see his vision through over time.

For me, the deal was all about having a goal—in this case, maybe an audacious one—and having the smarts and perseverance to see it through to success. It was never about how many zeros appeared on the bottom line.

To succeed, I had to present a plan that convinced Scott to step aside. What was in it for him? I gave him an opening. He could step in within six months and buy back the project from me at a half-million dollars over the amount I was paying. In return, I took over his obligation for the half-million in earnest money, and I kept the project alive. I gambled that Scott would never come up with the money.

I worked most the night and the next day pulling all the details together. Finally, it was 4:45 P.M. and we all showed up at the bank. Scott pulled up in his Porche convertible, wearing an Armani suit, sunglasses, cowboy boots, and carrying a cell phone. (Remember, it was 1988; cell phones were outer-space novelties.) Scott had his two lawyers with him. I had Don Campbell. The seller had his attorneys. One other person showed up, Steve Wellington and his attorneys. Quite an assembly of suits.

Who's this Wellington guy? I wondered. Meanwhile, Scott had ambled into the bank, taken an empty desk, and proceeded to plop his cowboy boots up on the desk. He pulled out his cell phone for a chat with some fellow business mogul…or his mother. Who knows? It was all show.

Scott was a deal junkie just like me. He liked the intrigue and the excitement. I told him, "Look, I'll give you $100,000 in cash just to get out of this deal and you're done with it. Or, you can buy me out for a half-million and what I have into it within six months."

He took that deal because he really wanted a chance to get back into the action.

These were 1988 dollars. Fast forward to 2010 and add three zeros. We're talking about a million and five million dollar sums at stake.

Scott was ready to sign the six-month deal when this new person popped up, Steve Wellington. "By the way," Steve said, "I have twenty-five percent invested in this deal. $250,000. Scott was my partner."

Scott had never mentioned Steve.

Steve was the smart Harvard grad who had worked with Mayor George Latimer of St. Paul on advising people at the state level on urban/suburban land use policy. Steve was just getting established in real estate development.

"Okay, Steve," I said, "my partner Jim Emison and I are going to be in this deal with seventy-five percent ownership of the property and you can stay in for twenty-five percent."

He wanted my personal guarantee that his investment was safe, and I wouldn't give him that guarantee: "What I can promise is that you're in the deal, and Jim and I are good for the money."

We closed at five P.M., and I went to work with Don Campbell doing the legal paperwork we needed to ensure that all the ducks were in a row. Clear title. Iron clad agreement. Scott had no say in the deal unless he exercised his option within six months. Steve started to see that we were serious, legitimate players and he became more comfortable.

That was the start of a twenty-year working relationship with Steve Wellington, the guy whose Wellington Management Company became one of the most respected in Twin Cities' real estate development. We went on to build more than thirty buildings together. I admire his careful, measured, and thorough approach to big, complex projects. I especially value Steve's ethical compass. He is not only a business partner, but also my close friend and confidante who I trust completely.

Scott Steindorf never exercised his option. Town Center was fully developed; the last time I checked (2009), its total market value was estimated at more than $30 million. Not bad for a farm kid from Ellsworth whose teacher told him he wouldn't get to first base. Amazing, too, how we hang on to hurtful comments from decades ago.

The year I made that eleventh-hour deal, I was named an Entrepreneur of the Year, a prestigious annual award given by *INC.* magazine and Arthur Young accounting firm.

A BRIDGE TO A NEW STAGE

If the business deals were my drug, sailing was my tranquilizer. In 1980 I bought my first sailboat—a thirty-nine-foot Morgan that I named Anne Marie. At first, I treated this new-found sport as a business. Very soon my "business idea" turned to love of the sea and sail. What followed was a parade of beautiful sailboats in my care, each larger and more beautiful than the one before. Three classy crafts all named after my daughter, Anne Marie, and my fifty-four-foot custom Hylas, built in 2002, that we named *Serenity*.

I took sailing lessons at the Offshore Sailing School, based on the island of St. Croix and run by the respected Annapolis Sailing School. As my skills expanded, so did my aspirations. I planned ocean crossings with my friends from the Decathlon Club. Though these crossings were challenging, requiring every ounce of good sense and stamina, they were also ripe for introspection. When the Atlantic wasn't blowing thirty knots and whipping up swells fourteen-feet high, my boat was a haven.

I will never forget our crossing from New York City, via Bermuda to the Caribbean. My friends and I talked about relationships. Newly divorced and recovering from compulsive overeating, I was dreaming of a healthy relationship that would finally last.

My buddies talked knowingly about the "stages" of relationships. Stage One was the period of lust and excitement; anything goes and your dreams are big. In Stage Two, things start to get mundane; you realize that everybody's human, but the relationship is still good. You do things together. You have fun. You're starting to get to know each other on a deeper level. Stage Three is pain. She's chewing your ass. She's trying to change you. If you're married, she's lobbying for a divorce so you can marry her. The relationship has become manipulative and destructive. Woman is the enemy. That's what my guy friends thought.

I'm listening and thinking, *That's not where I want to end up.*

I brought a book with me on that sailing trip, and I had plenty of time to read and reflect in the cockpit as I took the night watch. Written by Richard Bach, the book was called *A Bridge Across Forever*.

Bach talked about relationships that didn't have the Stage Three pain that my sometimes-cynical, older male friends described. Stage Three, as Bach described it, was the spiritual phase where a couple goes to a higher level. You grow individually. And you grow together.

Just as dawn was approaching, I saw the yellow glow on the horizon. Then I saw the bird, a tired songbird that had somehow been blown out to sea. For the bird to find us in the midst of the huge ocean was a miracle. The bird made a circle and dove toward our boat—and missed, tried again, missed again. Exhausted, the bird tried once more and descended, landing lightly on my arm. I gently picked up the bird and settled it into a corner of the cockpit with a dishcloth cushion and water. Three days passed and the little bird never left. When we finally approached land, the bird lifted its wings and climbed in the air.

That bird reminded me of commitment and perseverance. About going for what you need and getting it. I resolved to do the same.

SIX

THE THRILL OF THE CHASE

FINDING MY SOULMATE

"There's someone you just have to meet, Burt."

My first step in being out of the office and still in touch was at dinner in June 1988 at the Decathlon Club with Judy, a saleswoman who just outfitted me with a car phone, one of the first installed in the Twin Cities.

Judy's remark was a relief. I thought *she* was interested in me. I was just getting comfortable with the idea of dating and taking it slow. I was skiing with my guy friends in Vail and sailing in the Caribbean, and my business life was great. I didn't want anything to interfere with my healthy recovery.

Syble and I had divorced three years before, and I'd finally moved past the pain and regret of another failed marriage. I was still a little unsure of myself around women. I'd only had a few dates. Nothing serious. The woman I spent the most time with was a good friend I met at a "growth group" when we both were coming out of failed marriages. We leaned on each other during those difficult times. We cried together, and grew together, and even though she was attractive, our relationship was never romantic.

"Burt," Judy continued, "This woman is separated from her husband. She's beautiful; she's really nice." (Judy fancied herself a "yenta," so she loved making matches.)

Walking out to my car after dinner, Judy turned to me, grinning, and reached for my new phone. "Hey, Burt, let's go over there, now. Yvonne's house is on the way to my house. I'll call her and check it out."

"But, Judy, it's ten P.M."

Yvonne Lunderborg was snuggled under a coverlet with an absorbing novel. Her two young children, Brian, five, and Katie, nine, were tucked in for the night.

"Now, Judy?" Yvonne was incredulous, but Judy was insistent. She had tried to find a match for Yvonne before.

"You're going to like this one," Judy promised. "I swear. He's part of a 12-Step program, and you have your black belt in Al-Anon. He's athletic. He skis and sails. He's good-looking. It's Friday night. Get up! We'll be there in thirty minutes."

Yvonne reluctantly left her warm nest, washed her face, brushed her teeth, and smoothed her hair. She dressed as if she never had gone to bed. Yvonne had been separated from her husband for over three years. She promised herself to be open to new possibilities, even spur-of-the-moment meetings.

WE WERE A PERFECT FIT

Yvonne Lunderborg was single and beautiful, and she lived in a big house on the Mississippi River Boulevard in St. Paul. I didn't know anything more than that.

Judy left us and busied herself in Yvonne's kitchen. Meanwhile, Yvonne's kids peeked around the corner, studying me while we talked for thirty minutes.

Afterward, in the car, Judy programmed Yvonne's phone number into my cell phone. She promised her friend was interested.

I phoned Yvonne that same night and asked her to join me for dinner the next day. We agreed on a time—or so we thought. Yvonne had seven P.M. riveted in her brain. I had six P.M. Naturally, I was panicky, sitting at the Decathlon Club at 6:30 wondering if I was being stood up. Yvonne appeared at seven P.M. We laughed about the confusion, and from that day forward, I have seen or spoken to Yvonne every day.

Yvonne told me that most of her friends were compulsive like me. The ones in recovery had learned to harness their energy in a healthy, positive way. She said she grew up with friends who were vivacious and outgoing and she was the shy one, the peacemaker. She had years of experience in Al-Anon because her husband was an addict and her father was an alcoholic. She had learned to keep her unhealthy care-taking of others in check.

We were a perfect fit.

Yvonne says I "absorbed" her. I wanted to see her all the time, and she felt I wanted to be in control of our plans. She called it "steamrolling."

A few weeks after we met, Yvonne had a trip to the Wisconsin Dells with a girlfriend, so I invited myself along with my daughter Anne Marie. The whole thing was an awkward dance. Yvonne's friend couldn't go at the last minute and my ex-wife Syble didn't want our daughter traveling with me and another woman. Yvonne and I were left with her two youngsters in the Dells, she in one hotel room, me in another. I wasn't accustomed to dating, and during the night, I was so anxious I called my daughter Jennie at school in Madison, Wisconsin. I asked her to come to the Dells right away with her boyfriend, Matt. Apparently, I needed "reinforcements." I was out of my element, out of control, and I hated it. I even considered taking a Greyhound bus home.

I had a long way to go to learn how to function in a relationship as a sober adult. Fortunately, by the next day, things started to improve.

SEARCHING AND FEARLESS

This is a prime example of what happens to addicts when we get into recovery. We give up our drug of choice, but we have lots of work to do on our personal shortcomings and defects of character, as we call them in Overeaters Anonymous. These personal qualities usually caused the anxiety and fear that drove us to food, alcohol, drugs, gambling, shopping, or working incessantly in the first place. (They weren't the only factors that drove us to our drugs. Genetics and child-hood environment steered us to addiction, also.)

Trying to control everything is one of my big defects. In the first year of my recovery, I examined this shortcoming, and others, in detail. I wrote them all down and admitted the pain that my actions caused. When I looked at specific examples, I began to see patterns of control, manipulation, selfishness, dishonesty, and fear. Conducting this "searching and fearless moral inventory" was Step Four of my 12-Step program, and it was a tall order.

Most people have never taken a hard look at their lives and behavior in exacting detail. If you're Catholic, maybe you've done a little time in church confessionals. But most of us go through life just trying to get along, coping as well as we can, practicing the survival techniques we learned as children and young adults. If we grew up with a moral compass shaped by our parents or a faith community, we had a chance to make clearer distinctions between right and wrong.

I discovered that many addicts don't know what their values truly are. They spend so much time telling people what they *think* people want to hear that they lose themselves.

I somehow ended up with an acceptable value system, but all bets were off when I got scared. My natural instincts for self-protection and self-seeking kicked in, and I resorted to control, manipulation, and dishonesty to get what I thought I needed.

Doing my Step Four personal inventory was heartbreaking. I had to own up to the pain I caused other people and the pain I inflicted on myself. Equally hard was sharing my inventory with my sponsor. Out loud. Now I was on Step Five of the 12-Step program: "We admitted to God, to ourselves, and to another human being the exact nature of our wrongs."

Addicts keep lots of secrets. It's how we protect ourselves. Sharing things I was most ashamed of was excruciating. My meeting with my sponsor lasted hours, and I trusted her to keep everything confidential. She made no judgments. She was a willing, compassionate, and patient listener. She helped me re-discover my strengths and blessings, too. She urged me to take a good look and "own my assets." Addicts can be brutal with themselves. They usually need someone to tell them that they are lovable, after all.

My sponsor helped me see the patterns of behavior I used to protect my scared self. When it was over, I felt tremendous relief—as though I'd left decades of guilt and regret in some imaginary landfill. I didn't have to carry that garbage around with me anymore. I had nothing left to hide, and I was less fearful.

The biggest gift of Steps Four and Five was discovering that I didn't need to resort to these shortcomings and defects of character. Ever again. My 12-Step program is rooted in being honest, open, willing, and accountable, so my hurtful coping tactics are less powerful than they used to be.

Don't get me wrong, my "guilt dump" in the imaginary landfill in 1983 wasn't a once-and-for-all gesture. I try to resurrect my controlling, manipulating, and selfish ways because I'm human and flawed like everyone else. But here's the difference: When I do it now, I see the patterns. I recognize what I'm doing to myself and others. I have a choice. I can stop using these sick instincts of self-protection-gone-berserk, or I can choose not to act on them in the first place. If I'm really struggling, I call my sponsor, seek out a friend in the program, or talk to God.

TAKING THE BACKSEAT

Here's where faith comes in: faith in something bigger and more powerful than I am. I believe that a "higher power," who I call God, has my best interests at heart. I now know that *I am not* God, though I believed I was for years. I have faith that if I stay connected to God—every day—and do my part by "working" the 12 Steps, life will be better than I ever imagined: serene, peaceful, happy, joyous, and free. If I really ask, and mean it, God will remove the shortcomings and defects of character I've leaned on since childhood. They were my coping and survival skills. Sometimes I have to ask God many times a day to remove them. When I'm working a good recovery program, I simply don't need those old crutches anymore. That's what Steps Six and Seven are all about: being entirely ready to have God remove all my defects of character and humbly asking God to remove my shortcomings.

Even in the hard times of loss and disappointment, I know, to my bone marrow, that I'm not alone. I can cope, and I'll come out the other side of a crisis whole. No matter how bad things are. I mean the big stuff: deaths of family and friends, a cancer diagnosis, life-altering changes in my children's lives.

I know this because I've seen it in action for more than twenty-five years.

Ever since I got into recovery, I have held this recurring image: I'm riding a two-person bike, and I'm in the backseat. God is pedaling in front.

Steps Two and Three of my program focus on remembering who's in the driver's seat. In Step Two, I came to believe that a power greater than myself could restore me to sanity. For some people on the edge of recovery, that's impossible to imagine. They have played God all their lives, and because denial is a huge force in addiction, they don't believe their lives are out of control. Even if they drink to a blackout every night. Even if their first thought in the morning is calling their dealer. Even if they awake to empty potato chip bags, candy bar wrappers, and sticky ice cream cartons.

Two failed marriages, chronic sadness, and my bizarre behavior with food since age ten was enough to convince me of the insanity in my life. I was lucky. I believed in something bigger than me. Maybe I didn't go to church, but I could embrace a spiritual life by imagining God in the front seat of that bike. In Step Three, I made a decision to turn my will and my life over to the care of God, as I understood God.

At first, turning my life over may seem like a sign of weakness. But

I now see it as a sign of strength. For decades, I turned my life over to food, alcohol, speed, nicotine. When I got into recovery, I made a better choice about who I trusted my life to, and it's worked for me. Sure, I try to slip into the front seat—the driver's seat. I struggle with my self-will-run-riot. But when that happens, I try to slow down, reflect, and ask for help from God and others in my recovery program.

For habitual controllers like me, turning my will and life over to the care of God is an everyday, and sometimes every hour, practice, especially when my EGO steps in and Edges God Out. By the way, recovery is full of acronyms and pithy sayings like, "Easy Does It." Some people make fun of them, calling them simplistic drivel. Over time, I came to understand that those sayings are actually true and quite helpful.

Something happens to people in recovery before they're halfway through the 12 Steps. We call them "The Promises," and they promise this:

"If we are painstaking about this phase of our development, we will be amazed before we are halfway through. We are going to know a new freedom and a new happiness. We will not regret the past nor wish to shut the door on it. We will comprehend the word serenity and we will know peace. No matter how far down the scale we have gone, we will see how our experience will benefit others. That feeling of uselessness and self-pity will disappear. We will lose interest in selfish things and gain interest in our fellows. Self-seeking will slip away. Our whole attitude and outlook upon life will change. Fear of people and of economic insecurity will leave us. We will intuitively know how to handle situations which used to baffle us. We will suddenly realize that God is doing for us what we could not do for ourselves.

"Are these extravagant promises? We think not. They are being fulfilled among us—sometimes quickly, sometimes slowly. They will always materialize if we work for them." (*Alcoholics Anonymous: Big Book*, Fourth Edition, Alcoholics Anonymous World Services, Inc., 2001)

Though I never imagined all these promises coming true, they started happening during my first year of recovery and they've multiplied over the decades.

THE PROMISE OF YVONNE

One of these promises was Yvonne. In some ways, Yvonne and I had similar backgrounds. She grew up in a Scandinavian household and her dad, one of sixteen kids, was a Southern Minnesota farm boy. Her grandmother used to talk about having seven children serving in World War II.

Yvonne's father was an alcoholic who tried to find recovery in six treatment centers, but he never succeeded. He spent the last twenty years of his life in a sober house and, ultimately, in a Veteran's Administration home. He was an Archie Bunker type to Yvonne's Princess Grace, a completely dissonant father–daughter pair.

Yvonne is a natural beauty, so she landed modeling jobs even as a teenager. She had a wanderlust, too. She joined Northwest Airlines and flew all over the world for eleven years when "stewardesses" had to weigh-in before a flight, wear girdles, mini-dresses, and go-go boots—high fashion in the 1960s. She married at twenty-four, and she swore she'd never choose a man who took more than two drinks in an evening. Well, her husband didn't exceed the two-drink limit, but he made up for it with marijuana. No matter how much we swear we won't marry our fathers (or mothers), many of us do.

When we went to restaurants, Yvonne knew the bartenders and maitre d's. Who could forget beautiful Yvonne? She seemed so confident.

I carried my heavy insecurities inside me. But here's the good news. I had enough self-knowledge from my recovery program to tell Yvonne what made me insecure. Instead of being put off by it, she appreciated my honesty. I told her everything about me—the good, the bad, the nicks and warts. I over-explained myself and probably took my newfound openness to an extreme. But it was a defense, too. If I told Yvonne all about me, she'd have the truth up front and I'd know where I stood with her right away. Did we have a future together or not? I could count on Yvonne to be a straight shooter.

MELDING LIVES AND FAMILIES

My daughter Jennie had already left for college, and John would soon graduate from high school when Yvonne and I became a couple in 1988. That left my younger daughter, Anne Marie, with me part of the time. Yvonne's children, Katie and Brian, were about Anne Marie's age and spent time with us regularly, in keeping with Yvonne's joint custody arrangement. Our lives and families began to meld.

That first year, Yvonne sold her house on the Mississippi River Boulevard and bought the smaller one nearby that needed lots of work. In a gesture uncharacteristic of me, I helped her move into a place that looked like a tear-down in a high-class neighborhood. I had my high-tech townhouse with all its amenities in Hudson, Wisconsin. As we spent more and more time together, we used both homes. We included our children, and the shift from "her" children and "my" children to "our children" was gradual.

Yvonne loved to travel, but she needed to put down roots. She also needed to be married. I didn't resist. It was an easy position to take because she was still married. I *did* think she should move on, and I encouraged her to get serious about getting a divorce.

We had only known each other about six months when I invited Yvonne to come sailing with me. She had traveled to the Caribbean one year earlier with a group of friends. They anchored their luxury cruiser near the island of St. Bart's, and she walked a path along the ocean to Columbia Bay. The hike took Yvonne beside the coastline, the tropical air heavy with salt, ocean rollers carving the sand, golden light tinting the water. She sat on a little stone wall and saw a cluster of modest beach houses nearby. Someday, Yvonne thought to herself, I'll find my soul mate, and I'll bring him back here.

In early February 1989, we sailed into Columbia Bay together. We took that walk along the coast and, on February 12, I sat in the cockpit of my sailboat, reading my morning meditation from a little book I always carry with me. On that day, the message described what both of us hoped for: "Love is, above all, the gift of oneself."

Yvonne wrote a note in my book marking that day and giving me confidence that she believed she had found her soul mate. Her note was cryptic: "fulfills and surpasses Yvonne's fantasy at St. Bart's."

WE'RE PARTNERS, RIGHT?

As we grew closer, Yvonne and I dissected my need to control in many counseling sessions with our "uber-therapist." Ann was "neutral territory" for us both, and I couldn't charm or manipulate her with my elaborate rationalizations. I instinctively wanted to control Yvonne, and she had an overriding fear of being controlled.

My journals from our early years together are filled with notes that reflect our struggle to become a healthy "we": "YV thinks I'm trying to change her...that I can't accept her for what she is. I don't think she fully trusts me. How can I tell her what my needs are without YV feeling controlled? How are we going to become a 'we'?"

Along with counseling, we shared weekends together at the Hazelden Renewal Center, exploring what a healthy, intimate relationship meant to both of us. I was a total amateur. Had Yvonne met me before I got into recovery, she would have run the other way. As it was, I was only three years into my 12-Step life when our friend Judy matched us up. I don't think Yvonne had much experience with honest intimacy, either.

After living my life in controlled "boxes," I was only beginning to create a seamless life. Yvonne would not be put in a box—no how, no way—and her greatest fear was me "shutting the lid," dictating her choices, always taking the lead. Our therapist helped me see that.

I honestly didn't realize the depth of Yvonne's personal strength and independence. She was absolutely clear about her values; she wanted to retain her own bank account and direct her own investments. In my previous marriages, I was a steamroller and I got my way. I was tenacious. With Yvonne, any fantasies I harbored about changing her were futile. When I realized that, our relationship improved dramatically. Over time, we agreed to disagree on certain things and that didn't jeopardize our relationship. Just because we did something Yvonne's way, versus my way, did not mean I had "lost." We gave up the notion of winning and losing in our relationship, and we started to think like equal partners. Even now, when we hit a snag, the phrase that we repeat like a mantra is, "We're partners in this, right?"

Our therapist taught us "mirroring," a kind of active listening that involves acknowledging what each other says by paraphrasing what was just said, before putting in our two cents. It's respectful, and it opens up our minds and hearts to each other, even when we disagree.

Many years later, after Yvonne and I married in 1992, I came across notes that described what we began creating together on that first, magical sailing trip in 1989: "For me, home is not a physical place, but a place where love is. Whether it's St. Paul, Vail, Florida, or the boat, we always say, when we return to these places, 'We're going home.' As a child and young adult, I was always searching for home. I believe I first found home when I joined that circle of compulsive people in 1982. My soul longed for a place to belong, a place to be connected. My soul longed for love, and it longed for God."

I found love in Yvonne, our children, and our grandchildren. I found God in my recovery program.

SEVEN

GOING TO THE DOGS

DOGGONE IT!

Our Twin Cities sportswriters were salivating like race-crazy grey-hounds. They couldn't wait to see how far we'd come from a huge, weedy vacant lot outside of Hudson to a flashy $33 million racing complex. Some racing people called our track the best in North America. People like Patrick Reusse and Sid Hartman would fill lots of column inches with their insider stories and color. TV loved the images, and radio had plenty of race sound bites for dramatic effect. They all created the local buzz we needed for opening day.

I invited a platoon of reporters and sports celebrities to walk the unfinished venue and get the inside scoop on our high-visibility project. Then, we bused them down to St. Croix Marina for a paddleboat river cruise. We served them a gourmet sit-down dinner and answered all their questions, told a few stories, too, talked about the vision for grey-hound racing: how clean and fun it is for families, how good it is for communities, how successful this sport had been all over the country.

We pulled into the marina parking lot and faced a pack of people carrying homemade signs: "No Track for Hudson," "Hudson Going to the Dogs," "Not In My Backyard!"

Oops. The press knew this was a controversial project. They were used to covering opposition. At least these demonstrators didn't shout slurs.

We pulled away from the marina with a whistle from the paddle-boat captain. It's a gorgeous night: warm, sunny, dark-blue sky. Most everybody was on the rail, enjoying the scenery. Their view of the placard-carriers was receding, *thank God.*

We were well into our appetizers when two small planes buzzed us. Looking up, I understood why. Both were pulling banners shouting, "No Dog Track!"

It was enough to spoil my appetite.

Take a deep breath. Pass the paté.

Placards. Planes. Now runabouts were surrounding us, circling and shouting. They carried signs decorated with balloons and gaudy banners. They were like gnats that wouldn't go away.

A civilized dinner was out of the question. Our opposition was now front page news, not our stunning, new track.

MY WISCONSIN WAGER

I found the biggest challenge of my business career in a pack of greyhounds. The whole thing started when Wisconsin approved pari-mutuel wagering—a French term for betting in a group. When a person places a bet on a dog, a horse, or a race car, the money goes into a pool along with other betters. The house takes its percentage for handling the bets, and the winners divide the pool. A state that

Yvonne and me in St. Lucia on our
first sailing trip, 1988

With Barkley atop Mt. Holy Cross in Vail, Colorado

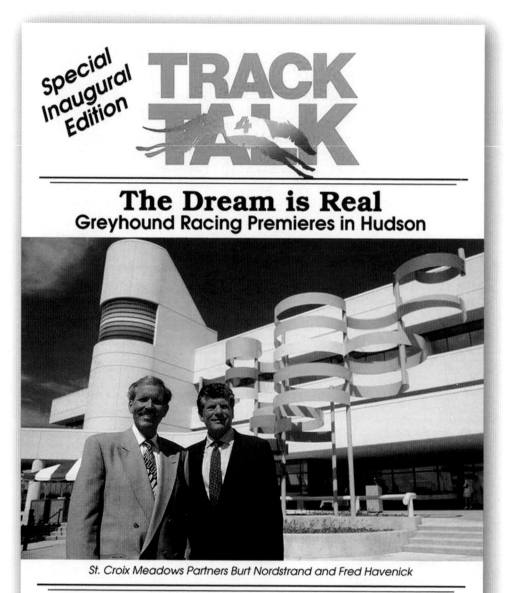

St. Croix Meadows Partners Burt Nordstrand and Fred Havenick

At our wedding in Vail: (L–R) Brian, Matt, John, me, Yvonne,
Katie, Jennie, and Anne Marie, 1992

Yvonne and me in St. Maarten on our
honeymoon, 1992

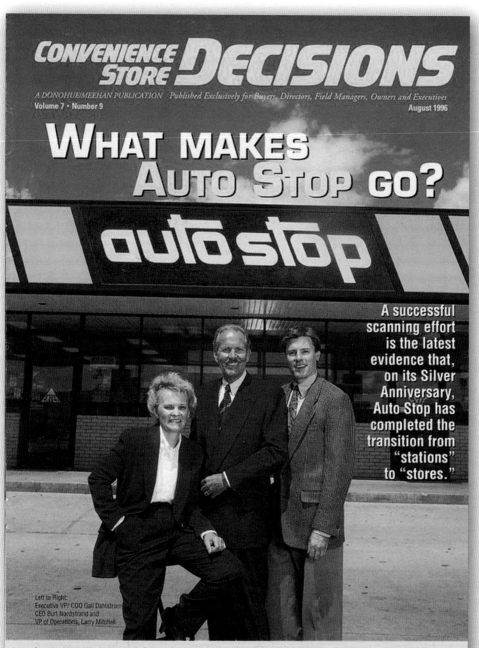

CONVENIENCE STORE **DECISIONS**

A DONOHUE/MEEHAN PUBLICATION Published Exclusively for Buyers, Directors, Field Managers, Owners and Executives
Volume 7 • Number 9

August 1996

WHAT MAKES AUTO STOP GO?

auto stop

A successful scanning effort is the latest evidence that, on its Silver Anniversary, Auto Stop has completed the transition from "stations" to "stores."

Left to Right:
Executive VP/ COO Gail Dahlstrom,
CEO Burt Nordstrand and
VP of Operations, Larry Mitchell

Operation Automation: Advice from the Software Doctors (p. 40) • How Fas Mart Makes Chicken Fly (p. 53) • Retooling the Candy Category (p. 22)

On Mom's 90th birthday: (L–R) Ron, Mom, Dennis, Gail, and me

Jim Emison and me aboard
Serenity in St. Barts (our
last sailing trip together)

Me on the top of Mt. Holy Cross

Family photo: (back) Jennie, Yvonne, me, and John:
(front) Anne Marie, Brian, and Katie, 2003

Jennie and me, 2003

John and me in British
Columbia for helicopter
skiing, 2007

Anne Marie and me in
San Francisco, 2005

Biking up Mt. Evans in
Colorado, 2009

Yvonne and me skiing
in Vail, 2008

Yvonne (60) and me (70) in St. Lucia celebrating our birthdays, 2009

Our grandchildren (L–R): Sam, Gabe (holding Murphy), Nick
(holding Samara), Ikey; (front) Seth, Sonny, and Michael, 2009

sponsors parimutuel wagering earns a percentage of all the betting activity—a painless, new form of revenue and an economic stimulus.

I didn't give greyhound racing or Wisconsin betting much attention, though gambling was once an outlet in my pre-recovery days. For me, gambling went the way of cigarettes, diet pills, alcohol, sugar, carbs, and compulsive overeating when I turned my life around in the late 1970s. I still gamble a bit in business, though I consider my gambles calculated risks. I never "bet the farm" on a single business venture, and I never will.

One ordinary day in August 1989, Fred Havenick, a tall, outgoing guy from Florida, arrived at my Hudson SSG headquarters unannounced with his colleague, Paul Lewin.

So began a six-year journey that ultimately ended up at the United States Supreme Court.

Fred was the son-in-law of Isadore Hecht, a big player in Florida's banana business and, at one time, Del Monte's largest shareholder. When Hecht sold his shares in 1953, he bought a run-down, greyhound racetrack in Miami and a second track in the Naples/Fort Meyers area. He turned them both into successful moneymakers. By the time I met Fred and Paul, the Hecht family business owned those two successful dog tracks and a large portfolio of real estate in Florida, Chicago, and elsewhere.

NO EASY TASK

Before calling on me, Fred and Paul met with a local realtor and identified a one-hundred-acre parcel for sale just over a mile south of Interstate 94—the only site in the city suitable for a greyhound racing track. But there was no ready access to the site from the freeway. Three large parcels and several houses stood in the way. They would have to acquire the land and move the houses to build an access road. On top of that, the potential track site needed an interstate cloverleaf and a four-lane divided highway to reach it.

Based on my experience in developing the downtown Hudson historic district and the commercial district on Hudson Hill, I saw tremendous real estate potential if this freeway interchange and four-lane highway were to be built. Obviously, a thirty-million-plus greyhound racetrack at the end of the road would be a powerful catalyst.

GREYHOUND RACING: A SURE THING

Fred and Paul believed in the good clean fun of greyhound racing. They told me about the family atmosphere at their tracks in Florida and the complete entertainment package offered to all ages every night of the week. They called greyhound racing the sport of the future—an exciting spectacle and lucrative investment.

At the time of their visit, there were fifty racetracks in the United States and twenty-five owners. Every track was successful. I asked if there had been any failures. They said that one racetrack in Las Vegas went belly up when a casino competed head to head with it. The upside potential was huge, they said: greyhound racing had become the fifth largest spectator sport in the United States and—because of their financial success—no existing tracks were changing hands.

The Hecht family had their eyes on Wisconsin. Fred and Paul were actively working with government officials and lobbying policymakers. They wanted to license, build, and run a track in Wisconsin.

Hudson was right next door to the Twin Cities of Minneapolis/St. Paul, a growing metropolitan area with a hard-working, affluent, and stable population. A greyhound track could easily draw Minnesotans who always demonstrated a healthy appetite for gaming. Even the State of Wisconsin went on record saying that Hudson was a likely site for a greyhound racetrack.

"How did you find me?" I asked. Fred and Paul already had connections in Wisconsin. They knew the opinion leaders next door in Minnesota, too, and they had contacted Tom Kelm, a highly visible political figure.

"If you want to get something done in Hudson," he'd said, "talk to Burt Nordstrand. He's the go-to guy."

Fred and Paul told me the Hechts were looking for someone who could put together a deal, someone with ethics and integrity, someone who could represent their interests in Wisconsin and be a local partner. The state required that any applicant for a greyhound racetrack must have a fifty-one percent Wisconsin ownership in the venture.

I was fascinated and intrigued. The more I thought about it, the more the attraction grew, stirring up the same kind of excitement I found in forbidden foods or the rush of putting together a complex real estate deal. I craved those feelings. The track and all it represented was intoxicating. Like a drug. I was well into my program of recovery and trying to live life a little gentler, so I had to give this massive commitment careful thought.

I also imagined what this project could do for Hudson—the town I had adopted as my own. This project could take Hudson to a whole new level of prosperity.

MY 800-POUND GORILLA

Honestly, the track absorbed my heart, soul, and mind for six years: every waking moment, many sleepless nights along with a few nightmares. It was the 800-pound gorilla of my career and the truest test of my recovery program. I was about to take my 12-Step program "on the road" and put it into practice in the most challenging and threatening circumstances. I risked dangerous depression when the controversy around the track became ugly or mountains of paperwork threatened to suffocate me. I got high on the recognition and adulation when the track opened to rave reviews. Now, I look at the weeds growing in the parking lot and it still makes me sad. I know I fulfilled my commitment, and I also know that Hudson is better off for my efforts because, track or no track, the acreage around Carmichael Road and Interstate 94 is generating millions in business revenue and taxes for the local communities. None of that would have happened without the track.

Through it all, my 12-Step program, Yvonne, my OA meetings, and my sponsor helped keep me sane. My sister Gail, Larry Mitchell, and our SSG staff kept my core company operating and growing. Bill Wanner skillfully managed BNA—Burt Nordstrand & Associates, my real estate division. Even though I had my hands full with the track, I always kept a hand in my main businesses. During this time, my secretary moved over to the track project and Kathy Ostlund entered my life as my executive assistant. She has been invaluable to me in all areas of my business and personal life. Like my recovery program, I have learned that no one is successful on their own. I count on others to help me, support me, keep me accountable and "right-sized."

The person who kept me centered and humble in the healthiest way was Yvonne. She was my stalwart, loving and passionate "corner man." After coming home from numerous six-hour hearings, she energized and patched me up for another day.

THE THRILL OF THE CHASE

Days after that first meeting with Fred and Paul, my son and I headed to Chicago to the annual American Hearing Impaired Hockey Association camp run by Stan Makita, a Hall of Fame Chicago Black Hawk hockey player. John hoped to win a spot on the U.S. Deaf Olympic Hockey Team (which he ultimately did in 1989).

Between watching John's games and coaching sessions that weekend, I had plenty of time in my hotel room to think. I pulled out my yellow pad and sketched the conceptual deal for the track—every legal and governmental step along the way, every key constituency we had to court. Who would join my team, what kind of support besides the financial commitment did I want from Fred, Paul, and the Hecht family? Where might we trip up, and how would I foresee it? What was the worst-case scenario? What was the best? How long would it take?

I asked myself the tough question: *was all this effort worth it to me? Would I do what was necessary to see this deal through to a successful end? Did I have the staying power?* No question. *But did I have the passion?* Yes, I wanted a challenge. Like the dogs, I always enjoyed the thrill of the chase. I had to balance this passion with my new lifelong commitment of abstinence and freedom from activities or substances that would threaten my life of newfound serenity.

That weekend, I formulated my vision for assembling the track property, building the freeway interchange and four-lane highway, and ultimately winning a license to build the greyhound track. Once I had my plan sketched out, I phoned Paul Lewin in Florida and walked him through it. I assured Paul that I had the ability to put together a team to assemble the property, win the license, and see the project through all the approvals necessary. Paul assured me that the only financial risk for me was obtaining the license. Once we succeeded, he and Fred promised the financing necessary to see the project through. I proposed a partnership where I would be the managing partner, and once we received the license, I would be safe from any financial risk.

A week later, I traveled to Miami with my longtime attorney, Don Campbell, and put together the written agreement between HAH Enterprises, the Hecht family's company, and my B.N. Investments. We formed Croixland Properties, the entity that would own the land and the racing facility known as St. Croix Meadows Greyhound Racing Track. We were equal partners.

MY DREAM TEAM

I assembled a first rate team of more than thirty professionals to support Croixland Properties: land engineers, architects, lawyers, lobbyists (a necessary evil), and the beginning of an office staff. I went to work accumulating the land and instructing our team to prepare drawings for my first informational presentation to the Hudson City Council. By August 1989, I had acquired all the necessary property. We contacted the state about designing and building a freeway interchange, and they supported it—as long we paid for it and we won the track license. In fact, they were willing to put our project on a fast track.

Our engineers worked with Hudson's engineers to design and

develop the four-lane highway leading to the proposed track location. It was a smooth process because the road was already included in the city's long-range plan.

With large colored sketches and drawings in hand, I made my way to City Hall to make my presentation to the City Council. I expected it to go like all the other previous projects I had done in Hudson: smooth sailing, unanimous support.

I WAS WRONG

When I reached the City Hall steps, I saw more than fifty protestors carrying homemade signs saying, "No Dog Track," "No to Gambling," "No to Animal Cruelty." The City Council chambers were packed. What I expected to be a short, welcome reception turned into a four-hour marathon as I listened to my opponents underscore the sins of what I thought was the most exciting project in Hudson's history.

The opposition had a full head of steam. They had organized as Concerned Citizens Responsible Development (CCRD) months earlier to oppose another track proposal, and now they turned their attention to St. Croix Meadows. The CCRD was a loosely organized group made up of several factions: those with legitimate concerns about increased traffic, noise, and lights; those in the Not-In-My-Back-Yard camp; some activists who supported no growth in Hudson, and others who were recruited and supported by gaming competition in the Twin Cities.

I knew I had to regroup when the chief of police insisted that I have an armed escort back to my office. I began the next day with more resolve than ever. I knew this project would not be easy, but I was also convinced it was the right project for Hudson and western Wisconsin.

I learned in my recovery program that I was responsible for the "footwork" of staying sober: going to meetings, praying, and working with my sponsor. The outcome of that effort was left to God. I approached the track the same way: do the footwork to the best of my ability and let go of the outcome, let go of the bad feelings of my opponents, let go of any anger or resentments I felt. I had turned my life over to God, and I was in the backseat of that imaginary bicycle. What worked in my recovery program would have to work in my pursuit of a successful greyhound track.

READY FOR PRIME TIME

Following that first meeting at City Hall, I realized the approval of our track proposal was not going to be based entirely on logic. It was going to be emotional, political, and sensitive. I needed to reinforce my team by adding a project manager, a financial manager, and saavvy public relations professional. I picked Tom Horner, the former chief of staff for a U.S. senator who had just left a large PR firm to start his own Twin Cities shop. Tom became my chief of staff, public relations advisor, and overall consultant. I had to learn how to sell our story to a variety of audiences—some friendly, some not; to give interviews when the questions weren't always soft balls, and to stay "on script."

During the next nine months, we worked at a furious pace. There were countless city council and planning commission meetings, public hearings, public relations events, and frequent dinners with Paul and Fred. Support for St. Croix Meadows Greyhound Racing grew, and we were in the local newspaper, on the radio, on TV in the Twin Cities and Eau Claire nearly every week with profiles, track stories, or updates.

Our opponents were vigorous and vocal, and I felt beat up at times. Even so, I never thought the harsh words were directed at me personally. No one was ambivalent about the track. You were either pro or con. Sometimes that feeling stretched to odd extremes. At one meeting, an opposing councilman was so frustrated before an important vote that he jumped out of the window at City Hall to avoid a quorum and the police went to fetch him and bring him back for a vote.

Here's the bottom line: the City Council supported our proposal by a four-to-two margin with strong support from Mayor Tom Redner.

The real heroes were local leaders who believed the project would benefit Hudson, and they said so, even when friends and neighbors were relentless in their opposition.

WHERE THERE'S SMOKE...

Finally the day came in May 1989, when our team and ten other applicants made the final appearance before the racing board in Madison. The meeting began at three P.M. on a Friday afternoon. After a few introductions and announcements, the board adjourned to make its final decision.

It was a nervous wait—like waiting for a jury to return in a high-profile murder trial.

All eleven applicant teams gathered in separate groups around a large auditorium, drinking bad coffee and analyzing our chances. One of the applicants was our closest geographic competitor, who partnered with Delaware North and wanted to build a track in Hudson Township.

Five hours later, at 8:15 P.M., the board chairman entered the room. He smiled and quipped, "Did you see the smoke in the chimney?" alluding to the white smoke that precedes the selection of a pope in Rome.

Racing board executive Terrence Dunleavy announced that all tracks approved for the five available licenses would be required to have an on-site adoption program for greyhounds that retire from racing. There was a pause followed by another long nervous pause.

"The following applicants will receive a license," Dunleavy finally said. Everybody on our team leaped up to hear the decision. The stakes were so high. It was a moment you can't imagine. St. Croix Meadows won, along with Wisconsin Dells, Lake Geneva, Kenosha, and Kaukauna.

The story was in every Wisconsin newspaper and the metropolitan dailies of Minneapolis and St. Paul.

There were public and private celebrations, including private dinners with Wisconsin Governor Tommy Thompson. It was a thrilling time in my life, but even in the midst of all that high-test attention and adulation, I held the principles of my 12-Step program close. By doing that, I could put my relationships with Yvonne, my family, and friends first in the face of the seductive and competing demands of this new venture. I had to stay abstinent and grounded in my lifelong recovery program. I couldn't risk a relapse into my old behaviors of self-will, self-centered thinking, manipulation, and dishonesty. If I did, I knew my dreams would shatter.

MORE HURDLES TO CLEAR

With news of the victory, Hudson Mayor Tom Redner said St. Croix Meadows would boost his city's $200 million tax base by an additional $100 million. The park would create 475 new jobs, and the total project could mean as many as nine hundred new jobs. Not to mention all the tourist dollars. Of course, not everyone in Hudson shared the mayor's exuberance. The opposition said the racing board acted illegally and ignored his group's request for a public hearing. He promised legal action.

In addition, a nasty rumor started making the rounds of Hudson: the Florida Hecht family was allegedly connected to a famous mobster, Meyer Lansky. I heard the rumor the day before a crucial council meeting, and we had to act fast. I called Florida and the Hecht's attorney, and my partners, Fred and Paul, flew up in a private jet the next morning. We all sat down with the Hudson city attorney and put his mind at ease. The rumor was groundless.

What followed next was fifteen months of lobbying, politicking, and rancor in Hudson. Just a month after the Wisconsin Racing Board awarded our license, the Hudson Planning Commission reaffirmed its original recommendation to rezone the site for the racing park. In July, the Hudson City Council issued our building permit. We bought the one-hundred-acre site and surrounding land necessary for the interchange and access highway. After more public hearings and extensive reviews, the Council again confirmed its decision to rezone the site for the park. On July 31, 1989, we were finally ready to start construction, but the opposition rallied.

Judge Thomas Barland ruled against their lawsuit to stop construction of St. Croix Meadows, and the judge also ruled that the City of Hudson acted legally. The anti-track candidates were shut out. The opposition was over.

By August 1990, construction finally started on Carmichael Bridge over Interstate 94 and the interchange ramps that would bring about ten thousand visitors weekly to St. Croix Meadows. Construction was underway for the racing facility.

We were on the fast track: within ten, short months we were open for racing.

MY PEAK EXPERIENCE

In early June 1991, we put the final touches on the $33 million racing facility; we won final racing board approval, and we planned "school racing" nights for the greyhounds to prepare them for opening night.

We held an open house on June 21 and a "Funny Money" night for a thousand people. Each guest had a couple thousand dollars of funny money to bet so they could learn about racing and wagering. We treated them to a one-hundred-foot long buffet, but I kept my distance from my "slippery" foods: any combination of fat, sugar, or salt.

The next day, June 22, was a red-letter day for me. Not only did we officially open St. Croix Meadows, but also I proposed to Yvonne.

We arrived at the track that night about one hour before post time, and Yvonne was stunning. She was definitely "queen of the track." There were satellite news feeds positioned and ready from every major metro television and radio station in Minnesota and Wisconsin. Newspaper reporters stood poised for the action to begin. They were all waiting for me to arrive. I was engulfed with requests for interviews. Both the Minneapolis and St. Paul metro dailies ran six-page color supplements featuring the track and opening-night festivities.

Eight greyhounds got the royal treatment when they were escorted to the starting post by "lead outs" or handlers wearing black tuxedos at 7:25 P.M. The first event was the Governor's Inaugural Race—post time 7:30 P.M.

The announcer shouted, "Here comes Wishbone." The mechanical lure that the dogs chase began to circle the track. They were all rockets right out of the gate. A crowd of 4,765 people wagered $362,490 for the first of thirteen races.

Minnesota Twins manager Tom Kelly, Twins player Kirby Puckett, and Timberwolves basketball players mingled with Governor Tommy Thompson, corporate CEOs, and average folks. A full orchestra played in the plaza entrance, and life-sized greyhounds carved in ice graced the buffet tables. We broadcast the event on closed-circuit TVs, using more than seven hundred strategically placed monitors throughout the park. People saw our track's "Adopt a Greyhound Program" complete our first two retired greyhound adoptions.

A PERFECT STORM

When we opened, St. Croix Meadows was the sixtieth greyhound racetrack in the United States. Our road to success seemed clear, but it wasn't.

The first sign of trouble was hearing a Wisconsin federal judge rule that Native Americans could offer gaming on their tribal lands if a state authorized a lottery.

The State of Minnesota rushed to enter into an unlimited gaming compact with its Minnesota tribes, while Wisconsin limited its agreements to six years. No one anticipated Las Vegas-type casinos. As time went on, Wisconsin renegotiated its compacts and the state eventually received millions of dollars in annual revenue. Minnesota remained locked into their permanent compact and its citizens received nothing.

In August 1991, Fred, Paul, and I made our way over to Mystic

Lake Casino located just southwest of Minneapolis. As we pulled up to the parking lot, I knew we were in trouble—the huge lot was full of cars and a 50,000-square-foot tent had been quickly built with flashing neon lights advertising the casino. On the opposite end of this massive parking lot were large construction vehicles working on the foundation of an equally massive permanent casino.

We were shocked when we walked into the temporary tent. It was packed with slot machines, blackjack tables, and people waiting in line to get their turn at the action.

I was quickly reminded of an old gambling truism: dog tracks beat horse tracks and casinos beats dog tracks. People gravitate to the fastest gaming action. Casinos were about to trump us.

Through that first summer and the next year, racing at St. Croix Meadows was fun, but we weren't meeting projections and our customers were going to Native American casinos.

There were other blows, too. The U.S. slogged through a deep recession that started with a major stock market crash in 1989 and culminated in major job losses, corporate downsizing, and business failures in the early 1990s.

Our track had opened during a once-in-a-lifetime sports era for the Twin Cities. Within twelve months, Minneapolis hosted the World Series, the Super Bowl, the NCAA basketball Final Four, the U.S. Open golf tournament, and the NCAA hockey finals.

As if that wasn't enough, Minnesota and Wisconsin were nearly smothered in twenty-six inches of snow when a Halloween blizzard crippled both states. Months of digging out and nasty weather made it hard to convince patrons that greyhound racing was a year-round sport in this climate. We weren't alone with bad news. All five of the Wisconsin dog tracks failed to reach their betting projections for 1991, and four of us projected losses at the end of the racing season in December. Everyone blamed the economic recession, competition from tribal casinos, and riverboat gambling.

OUR SURVIVAL STRATEGY

By the summer of 1992 our best chance for survival surfaced. We began talking to the St. Croix band of Chippewa Indians who operated an Indian casino in Turtle Lake, Wisconsin, approximately fifty miles from Hudson. We proposed partnering with them and adding casino gambling to our existing park or adjacent to it. The deal hinged on approval from the local Bureau of Indian Affairs (BIA) and its federal counterpart. Governor Tommy Thompson, the Wisconsin State Racing Board, and the gaming commission also had to bless the plan.

By the time we announced exploratory discussions with the St. Croix band of Chippewa, our track was surrounded by thirty-nine casinos in Minnesota and Wisconsin.

Déjà vu. The pro-track and anti-track caucuses rallied again in Hudson. More than three hundred people packed the Hudson City Hall in August 1992, when the City Council held a public hearing and the newly elected council voted four-to-two to oppose our plan to combine casino gambling and racing.

Not everyone was happy with the council taking a stand for the whole community. Citizens circulated a petition to authorize a referendum on a simple up or down question: "Do you support St. Croix Meadows merging with the St. Croix Band of Chippewa Indians and installing a casino at St. Croix Meadows Greyhound Racing track?"

More than six hundred people signed the petition, and the referendum was held on December 3, 1992. A majority of voters said they favored the plan. With the positive results of the referendum, the St. Croix Band of Chippewa was optimistic about getting the okay from the BIA and Wisconsin's governor.

Meanwhile, back at tribal headquarters in Turtle Lake, our potential new partners were having second thoughts. There was talk of a split between the tribe and their managing partners. They told us they had their hands full trying to operate their own casino in Turtle Lake and they couldn't honor with the partnership agreement with St. Croix Meadows.

We got the bad news in December 1992, and Fred Havenick decided he wanted to continue looking for an alternative. Fred and I discussed his plan, and after a lengthy discussion, I decided it was time for me to step aside. Continuing this work would be detrimental to my relationship with Yvonne, with my family, and to my lifelong recovery program. The more I reflected on this decision, the clearer the message: Some things are simply not meant to be.

In the next few days, I held a press conference and reported that my work at St. Croix Meadows was complete. I had spent six years of my life on this project and didn't regret a moment of it. We had kept our commitments in every way. It was time for me to settle into a more normal life that included building my existing business and focusing on my most important personal relationships.

In August 1993, Fred announced that he had a new agreement with a trio of Indian partners from northern Wisconsin. They were poor tribes hoping to make the lives of their people better. Next came the long road of review and, hopefully, approval by the local BIA, the Department of the Interior, our governor, the Wisconsin Gaming Commission, and the Wisconsin State Racing Board.

As the next year unfolded, Governor Thompson announced that

if the BIA would approve the combined track and casino project, he would not oppose it. The local BIA approved the plan and recommended it to its higher office in Washington. Of course, there were forces in Minnesota and Wisconsin that privately opposed the application. A coalition of seven tribes in Minnesota operated some of America's most lucrative gaming casinos, and those wealthy tribes didn't want new competition—especially from a project just a few miles from the Minnesota border.

FOLLOW THE MONEY

We heard disturbing news about a grocery bag of cash being handed over to then President Clinton's aide when he visited Minnesota. Within a few days of that alleged event, the BIA, run by Interior Secretary Bruce Babbitt, turned down our application. It was the first time in history that the federal BIA rejected an application approved by one of its local bureaus.

Rumor about the bribery incident made it into the media. The U.S. Senate held hearings, and these spawned a Department of Justice probe into the denial of our application. The Attorney General approved a special prosecutor to investigate. Bruce Babbitt was considered a model of integrity, but the details that came out were damning. Two of Babbitt's aides played critical roles in the application rejection. They quit the Interior Department and went to work for the very tribes lobbying to kill our project. Babbitt's former colleague and an old friend Paul Eckstein testified under oath that Babbitt said White House politics and huge campaign contributions from Indians influenced the BIA's decision.

Fred and the three tribes continued their battle. They appealed the BIA decision to the Western Wisconsin federal judge. The judge reopened the case because she believed there was undue political influence in the applicant's rejection. Four years passed and the judge approved a new application to be submitted to the Federal Bureau of Indian Affairs. Finally, by 2002, the BIA, and an entirely different staff than from the time before, reviewed the new application and approved it on February 10, 2002—seven months after St. Croix Meadows greyhound racing track closed.

For Fred Havenick, it was a moral victory. He fought a tremendous battle, but fate pounded the final nail in the coffin. In 2002, just two days after newly elected President George W. Bush named Wisconsin Governor Tommy Thompson his new secretary of the Health and Human Services, our approved application from the BIA arrived in the Wisconsin governor's office. Scott McCallum, Wisconsin's new governor, vetoed the application. His power to veto the BIA decision was upheld in the United States Court of Appeals for the 7th district in Chicago. Finally, on January 10, 2005, the case was appealed to the U.S. Supreme Court, but the court chose not to hear it.

My friend Fred Havenick kept trying to win approval of a casino in one of the Hecht family tracks, but he never got the opportunity to pull the handle on the first slot machine. He died of a fast-growing cancer in 2006 at the age of sixty-two.

The Hecht family still maintains St. Croix Meadows, but on a very limited basis. In 2009, it was twenty years since the project began. The story of St. Croix Meadows and what will become of that empty "field of dreams" is not over. But I have turned it over to forces beyond me.

EIGHT

FEEL THE FEAR AND DO IT ANYWAY

MY PEAK EXPERIENCE

About four A.M. in early August 1993, Barkley and I set out from our condo in Vail for Mount Holy Cross. We filled up on healthy carbs and protein in preparation for our first ascent of Colorado's best-known "14er," a 14,000-foot peak on every American climber's list of favorites.

Mount Holy Cross means a lot to me because I see it every day I ski Vail. On the east side of Holy Cross, the snow gathers in crevices and forms a clearly defined cross on the granite face. When the first climber discovered it more than 150 years ago, he said the unique snow formation was a beacon and a symbolic promise from God right in the middle of the American continent for all to see. The poet Longfellow wrote about Holy Cross:

> There is a mountain in the distant West
> That, sun-defying, in its deep ravines
> Displays a cross of snow upon its side.

161

In the early 1900s, Christians took pilgrimages there. It remains a magnet for hikers who want to climb every one of the 14ers in Colorado. I take the trek seriously, and safety is paramount. Every year, a half-dozen hiking parties get lost on the tricky descent and some are never found. Holy Cross can make its own weather, and dangerous storms materialize fast. A trip like this takes about ten hours at our pace. I planned it well.

I packed lots of water, extra food, and warm clothes. When we reached the trailhead outside of Leadville, Colorado, it was five A.M. and the faint glow of a sunrise warmed the eastern sky. Our hike first took us up a thousand feet, then down a thousand feet, then back up another five thousand. The final ascent at about thirteen thousand feet went up a final thousand where we scrambled on all fours over scattered boulders in thin, lung-searing air. On top of Holy Cross, the whole space was no bigger than a tennis court.

This trek was tiring and required perseverance, especially for a "flatlander" from Minnesota where the average elevation is below one hundred feet.

Barclay is half-shepherd and half-husky. Though he's a dog with a dark side, Barclay is my devoted canine buddy. He's just as independent as I am, and he hates being controlled, just like me. We're attuned to each other. Imagine walking through an airport pulling a dog crate and a roller bag, with a dog to manage, too. Even without a leash, Barclay always follows close behind me, regardless of the distractions, crowds, and car traffic. On the mountain, Barclay never leaves me and he tackles the trail with the gusto of a trained athlete.

It was a rush reaching that mountaintop for the first time in my life. But Barclay and I savored it for only fifteen minutes because clouds rolled in and a helicopter patrolling the peak warned us to leave soon. We moved fast on the descent, not forgetting the last stretch: one thousand grinding feet, uphill.

Nothing worth doing ever comes easily.

WE NEVER WALKED AWAY

Marrying Yvonne Lunderborg should have been easy. Except for me. After two failed marriages and years of active addiction, the promise of a healthy relationship in sobriety still seemed beyond my reach. *When*, I wondered, *would I screw it up with a relapse into my old ways? When would Yvonne get fed up and leave me?*

Even with the success of building the Hudson dog track, SSG's uninterrupted growth, and my lucrative real estate deals, I still lived with my old fears of not measuring up. *To whom?* Dad was dead.

While I enjoyed healthy recovery, going to regular OA meetings, calling my sponsor, and taking daily, quiet time with my Higher Power, I still felt like damaged goods, some of the time.

I was nine years sober in 1990 when Yvonne gave me a deadline. She was kind, but firm.

"Burt," she said, "I'm one of those women who not only *wants* to be married, I *need* to be married. Call me Sadie, Sadie Married Lady. That's what I want to be. Why not take a year, think about it, and give me your answer. We can continue living as we have, sharing our homes and traveling together. But if your answer is no, I need to move on. If someone else comes along, I'm going to be open to a new relationship."

Yvonne's declaration didn't come out of left field. We participated in shared counseling sessions to give our relationship the best chance of success. I was the consummate controller, and Yvonne rejected my control moves like the unwanted overtures from some adoring drunk. We battled over the smallest things: what each of us chose to wear, what we fixed for meals, stupid stuff that was simply emblematic of our struggle to be healthy and intimate together. Neither of us had any experience with healthy pairing. We were shell-shocked from decades of bad relationships with spouses and parents.

Here's the difference. When we fought, neither of us walked away. We still did our morning readings together, and we agreed to keep going to our therapist. We attended our 12-Step meetings: me to OA, she to Al-Anon.

When Yvonne spoke honestly about what she wanted, I was scared of losing her and terrified of damaging our relationship. I thought a lot about it and talked to my sponsor and close friends. I asked God to guide me.

The suspense was over when I felt the fear and acted anyway. I asked Yvonne to marry me in June 1991. We bought land and planned a new home in Hudson, and kept Yvonne's vastly remodeled home on the Mississippi River Boulevard in St. Paul. We traveled more to Vail where we skied, and in the summer, I hiked and biked in the mountains while Yvonne played golf.

We decided to marry in Vail on January 4, 1992, with only our family in attendance. We decided to announce the "done deal" to our friends the next day through faxes, mailed announcements, and phone calls. We wanted our moment to be private, small, and sacred.

Leading up to that day we had plenty of drama. On my birthday, December 13, a month before our wedding, Yvonne and I skied Vail Mountain. We planned to meet with a minister that same day in preparation for our wedding. On our last run down the mountain, feeling truly elated and excited beyond words, I lost my focus and fell hard. Yvonne hurried over and said I looked like "a yard sale"—skis, hat, gloves, gear strewn all over the slope. Then she looked closer; I was dazed and dopey. "What day is it?" she asked.

"I can't remember."

Burt, it's your birthday. "Who am I?" she insisted.

"I know that one," I grinned. "You're my honey."

I wasn't far from the chairlift so, with Yvonne's help, I limped over to the lift and rode down. We found the nearest emergency room. The doc told me my head was okay, but I had broken my leg and it would take six weeks to heal. Our minister came to the emergency room to meet with us.

I would not let anything, even a splintered tibia, interfere with our wedding. I had a removable cast for our ceremony, and we rode in a horse-drawn carriage through soft, falling snow to a picturesque Vail chapel. We gathered in the chapel basement before the service and entrusted our daughter Anne Marie with the ring. Just before we prepared to walk down the aisle, Anne Marie gasped, realizing she didn't have the ring. She raced back downstairs and returned, red-faced, but relieved. Another pre-wedding crisis averted.

All our children witnessed the event. Only a few hours earlier, I had defied the doctor and taken a turn on my skis, relying on my ski boot as a "cast." Chalk that one up to classic addict behavior.

Yvonne and I spent our first honeymoon night in the Vail Athletic Club, my home away from home, while our kids stayed in our condo. It was all perfect, until the next morning.

SAY WHAT?

I was up first, feeling nervous, anxious. My gorgeous wife and best friend was luxuriating between the sheets, while I sweat bullets at the kitchen counter.

What have I done? (I'm scared.)

I can't do this. (I'm not good enough.)

This whole thing is going to blow up in my face. (I'm hopeless.)

I want out.

Yvonne came into the kitchen and watched me pace.

Half-joking, she said, "You know, Burt, we've known each other four years now, but we can always get it annulled if you want to."

Silence.

"Would you put that in writing?"

I heard the thunder: that empty space where words hang suspended. They explode. They radiate fear.

I mumbled something about my lawyer and said I'd be back.

Alone in our honeymoon suite, Yvonne drew a bath and called Barbara, my longtime therapist. In tears, she explained the scene and Barbara's first words were, "Oh that poor baby. He is SO scared."

Over the sound of water running, Yvonne barked, "Hey, Barbara, what about me?"

Fortunately for both of us, that little melodrama lasted only a few hours. Rather than call my lawyer, I called my sponsor. Instead of running scared, I took the gondola up to the top of Vail Mountain where I had a clear view of Holy Cross Mountain. I asked God for help.

THE COMMITTEE LIES

In recovery, I finally understood what it really means to be a friend. Anyone who is deep in his disease of addiction cannot be a friend. We are self-centered and self-seeking. The people we called "friends" were often our using buddies. We used them and they used us. Together, we used our drug of choice and convinced each other that life was normal. Addicts drink together, drug together, womanize (or chase guys), gamble, and eat to gluttony together. We work ungodly hours together if we're workaholics. All we usually have in common is our shared drug. When the drug disappears, these friends often disappear, too.

I knew nothing about intimacy, with women or men, until I got into recovery. Why? I couldn't see beyond myself and my own selfish needs. I manipulated people. I used them. When they were no longer of use, I moved on emotionally. The people who mattered most to me—my family, close friends, and long-term employees—were largely unaware of my secret addicted life.

Now I know that friendship is about being honest, open, willing, and consistent, even when I'm afraid, confused, or overpowered by those nagging voices in my head. I call them "the committee." They tell me to take the easier, softer way out of problems. They say it's okay to lie *this* time. They convince me to hide out and isolate myself. They condone manipulation because I'm justified. They say my drug isn't all that dangerous and I deserve it because I worked so hard, because life is throwing me a curve, because I've had a killer day (week, month, year), because the people I love aren't doing what I want them to do.

My "committee" says love is an illusion and people don't really care about anyone but themselves. The "committee" lies. But sometimes I listen.

I liked what a morning reading (*Today's Gift*, Hazelden Foundation, 2009) said about this: First a quote by Eric Hoffer, "We lie loudest when we lie to ourselves." The reading continued, "When we're not honest with others, we're not being honest with ourselves. In recovery, we're taught how to heal our hearts. We admit we are wrong, and we do it quickly. We let our spirit speak out. We listen to our spirit and we let it have the loudest voice. This way, lies lose power over us. We find a way to be true to our spirit."

NUT CASE OR EARLY BIRD?

Yvonne taught me volumes about honesty and true friendship. So did Tim and Steve.

For years, I attended my Overeaters Anonymous meeting on Monday nights, but I was still the only man there. "Where are the other guys?" I wondered out loud to my recovering friend, Ellen.

"There's a meeting in St. Paul on Saturday mornings at 7:30," she said. "They call themselves the Early Birds, and there are several men that go. Let me give you a name and number, and you can call one of them."

When I called Steve, a successful Twin Cities attorney, he thought I was a nut case. His words: "Burt calls me from Vail, Colorado, and he says he's reaching out to other men in his 12-Step program. He tells me about his home in Vail and his sailboat in the Caribbean. We start talking boats first, then I tell him about the Saturday morning OA meeting in St. Paul and invite him to come. Honestly, when I got off the phone, I thought Burt was just some grandiose, loosely wired guy I'd never hear from again."

I went to the 7:30 A.M. meeting and identified myself as a newcomer to Early Birds, but not to OA. At the point in the meeting where people introduce themselves if they're willing to be a sponsor, a tall, clean-cut guy named Tim spoke up. I sought him out after the meeting, and Tim introduced me to Steve. *Oh,* Steve thought, *so you're the guy.*

Since that meeting eight years ago, Tim, Steve, and I have talked daily, as long as we're in cell phone range. Maybe just leaving messages, but checking in nonetheless. We share our struggles, our families, our work, our food slips. We ask each other for help. No topic is off limits. We marvel at the "little miracles," the happenings that are never accidents.

Tim runs his own highly successful real estate appraisal company, and Steve is a retired lawyer. All three of us have full lives, thanks to our recovery. Tim says we are close because we "fly at the same altitude." We have similar life experiences and history.

We recognize that even though we're older, wiser, and sober, trouble still finds us. We still worry, fret, and struggle. We also share our joys in equal measure. I will never forget reaching the summit of Holy Cross with Tim and sitting down to have a two-person 12-Step meeting at 14,000 feet.

Here's the promise: we know that we will be in each other's lives until the very end, even when we get old, crotchety, and stupid. That's what friendship in recovery means. It's built to last.

SERENITY AT SEA

Many of my true friendships have been forged on the water. I had not yet found recovery from compulsive overeating when I bought my first ocean-going sailboat in 1980. Twenty-eight years into recovery and three sailboats later, my friends and family could see me at my most peaceful and centered aboard my sailboat, *Serenity*. My boat is my haven in the Caribbean, and besides my cell phone, the only electronic gear on board is dedicated to navigation, VHF calls to marinas, water depth, speed, and wind direction.

Life is simple. Our sailing playground is the two-thousand-mile area from the British Virgin Islands to Venezuela. I start each morning with a reading from my meditation book, and even my friends who aren't practicing a 12-Step program like to participate. I make sure that no guest feels obliged to join me in the cockpit at sunrise. Recovery is a program of attraction, not promotion.

Sailing has plenty of parallels to recovery. I have a recovery coin that I keep with me. It has a sailboat etched on one side with the words, "We cannot direct the wind, but we can adjust our sails." On the other side of the coin, it says, "Powerless, but not Helpless." Living on a sailboat is simplicity at its best, and I am reminded of how little I need to be truly happy. Mother Nature's whims tell me how powerless I am. Being this close to natural beauty amplifies my closeness to God.

Especially on "dog watch" from midnight to four A.M. alone in the cockpit, I am convinced of my eternal connection to my higher power. Miles from land with ocean all around me, I know I am in the care of God.

Sailing also doles out frequent lessons in humility. I don't have all the answers. I still have a lot to learn. Mistakes are teachable moments. My "defects of character"—notably control—show up in neon.

Talk about the arrogance of an addict. I bought that first sailboat in 1980, before I knew how to sail. My friend Jim Emison told me about a guy in St. Maarten in the Caribbean who wanted ten investors to buy ten sailboats, put them in a charter fleet, and let them generate income while each investor got a tax deduction for the purchase (that's when the IRS allowed such things). I should have known the deal was a little shaky when the salesman flew to a Michigan ski lodge in a private jet to meet me and get my check a few days before yearend. His company was desperate for revenue.

LESSONS IN HUMILITY

That was when I decided I better learn to sail. Syble (my wife then) and I had gone to St. Croix in the U.S. Virgin Islands for a basic sailing and navigation class offered by the Annapolis Sailing School. We both earned certificates—me, as a captain, she as crew—and we boarded our new boat, named after our one-year-old daughter, Anne Marie. For several years, I worked hard to learn the fundamentals of good seamanship and I invited trained captains to join me as on-the-water coaches. Over time, I built my confidence, sometimes learning from classic mistakes: a hard-sided dinghy that flipped in heavy ocean swells; an outboard motor submerged in sea water; an anchor dragging along the sea bottom that put my sailboat at risk; lines from a sail fouling the main motor's propeller; a dead engine; a drifting sailboat; a ripped sail; nights alone in the cockpit while my friends slept down below, worrying that our anchor wouldn't hold and we'd drift God knows where.

I learned that one calamity—usually caused by inattention—can lead quickly to another and then another. Mistakes multiply with the intensity of building ocean swells. Now, that's humbling.

But for all its challenges, ocean sailing gives me some of the most memorable and peaceful times with friends and family that I have ever known. We live in close, but comfortable quarters. We share unforgettable experiences and vistas. We solve problems together, soldiering through a sudden squall or navigating a reef-strewn passage. All of these things build strong bonds. Together, we are fully, completely, unabashedly ourselves.

My first sailboat was my training craft, and the ten-boat charter fleet never paid off as the investors imagined. Most of them got out, but I traded my thirty-nine-foot Morgan for a forty-seven-foot Sparkman Stephens sailboat in 1985 that I named *Anne Marie 2*. She was moored in Fort Lauderdale, still without a mast and rigging. I had hired George, my coaching captain, a seasoned sailor from England, to oversee preparation of the boat for ocean cruising. We call it "commissioning." The project took about a month, and we exceeded my budget—as most boat projects do. When *Anne Marie 2* was finished, George and his wife, Sylvia, sailed *Anne Marie 2* up the east coast to Baltimore on the Chesapeake Bay where I invited friends to join me on get-to-know-the-new-boat cruises.

Anne Marie 2 was a knock-out by maritime aesthetic standards. As I became more comfortable as a skipper, we ventured up to Atlantic City and anchored just offshore from the Trump Towers. We sailed into New York Harbor and moored at Staten Island, a block away from the famous ferry, with an unforgettable view of Manhattan. We hired a limo to drive us around the hot spots, and when we arrived in front of fashionable P.J. Clarke's bar and restaurant, people thought I was Ted Turner (I wore a mustache then). The hostess gushed, "Right this way, Mr. Turner," and I didn't correct her.

We visited the famous Rainbow Room in Rockefeller Center wearing white pants, boat shoes, navy jackets, and no ties. The stuffy host looked sideways at us and muttered, "What did I do to deserve you guys? I've got men in here wearing thousand-dollar suits, and you don't even have socks on."

My friend Jerry had a quick, effective answer: "Maybe not, but we have a million-dollar boat out in New York Harbor."

He seated us.

We cruised along the coast of Long Island, then headed north to Cape Cod and Newport, Rhode Island, home of the most beautiful "boat flesh" on the East Coast and port for many retired America's Cup challengers. From Newport, we sailed our first ocean crossing: an eight-day, thousand-mile trip through the Atlantic Gulf Stream to Bermuda.

I had many years of thoughtful introspection aboard *Anne Marie 2*, especially during my dogwatch shifts. I loved that boat.

But as any sailor will tell you, we inevitably dream of a bigger boat. More space. More speed. More convenience. Around 1998, with Yvonne's help, I began shopping for Anne Marie's successor, but found nothing to compare. Instead, I invested in a total retrofit of Anne Marie 2 down to her bear hull at a cost of $600,000. She was a brand new boat, and we named her Anne Marie 3.

Halfway through that project, my captain, Russell Rogers, handed me a brochure for a breathtaking fifty-four-foot Hylas that had just been introduced at the Miami boat show.

My heart stopped. This was it. She looked like a big sister to *Anne Marie 3*, just as beautiful, just as sound with forty percent more space and length. I bought her with the understanding that her design (all custom) would take two years to build in Taiwan. Yvonne and I, along with Russell and his wife, Evelyn, planned every cupboard, seating arrangement, the stateroom, and special feature down below. All of us traveled to Taiwan several times to watch her progress. Russell and Evelyn spent a couple months there, supervising construction.

When I met Russell and Evelyn more than twenty years ago, I knew I had a couple I could trust to be the "guardian angels" and co-captains of my sailboats in my absence. They were Brits who lived in South Africa for twenty-five years. The heartbreak and unrest of apartheid moved them to build a sailboat and prepare it for their first ocean crossing. They converted their assets to gold and silver and set sail from their home country, not sure they would make a safe passage or see their grown children again. Tough, resilient, and resourceful, they crossed the Atlantic with a plan to sail around the world. When they saw the beauty of the Tobago Keys in the Caribbean, they decided it wasn't going to get better than this. The beauty of the Grenadines seduced them, so they took a break and decided to look for work. About the same time, I was searching for someone trustworthy in a region where a lot of locals make promises, but often, don't deliver.

I hired a local agent in St. Lucia, and word travels quickly in the Caribbean. Soon I was interviewing Russell and Eve. I had received a good report, and when Russell called, I asked him a single question.

"Do you smoke?" I asked Russell.

"No."

I hired Russell and Evelyn on the spot.

While our new boat was being built in Taiwan, Yvonne and I sailed our re-fitted *Anne Marie 3* down the Intercoastal Waterway to Florida, through the Bahamas, past Puerto Rico and the Dominican Republic, to the U.S. and British Virgin Islands, then down to Venezuela, with many stops at St. Maarten, St. Lucia, Antigua, and Grenada. We covered more than fifteen hundred nautical miles together.

As if getting to know each other on land isn't enough, there is nothing to rival two people sailing through the challenging, shallow waters of the Bahamas and across wide open waters to distant islands.

We learned to be a good team taking on every oceanic challenge that Mother Nature and the Caribbean obstacle course of coral reefs dealt us.

We took delivery on our new boat in 2002, and in honor of my recovery, I named her *Serenity*.

CUNNING, BAFFLING, POWERFUL…AND PATIENT

People ask me why I still go to OA meetings after twenty-eight years of recovery. I'm sure they pose the same question to members of AA (Alcoholics Anonymous), NA (Narcotics Anonymous), ACA (Adult Children of Alcoholics), and Al-Anon. The answer is the same for all of us: if we skip meetings, we forget that we are lifetime addicts or we forget how the addicts in our lives continue to affect us. We never get well; we just have a daily reprieve based on following our 12-Step program.

For people who love addicts (whether they're in recovery or not), they need a reminder to take care of themselves and give up any illusions about "saving" or changing the people they love.

Addiction is cunning, baffling, powerful, and patient. Here's a perfect example. Many years before I confronted my compulsive overeating, I gave up caffeine because it hyped me up, made me anxious, and robbed me of sleep. Fifteen years passed without taking any caffeine. Then I was skiing alone in Vail. Yvonne and I had just married. Our relationship was solid. All my business ventures were proceeding well, even in the midst of the early 1990s' recession that rocked the United States. I had a full, satisfying, and successful life. I had no compelling reason to pick up an old "drug."

Even so, I took a break from skiing in the Vail Mountain cafeteria and started sipping Diet Coke while I waited for my sandwich. It was my first caffeine in years. After lunch, I was a better skier. More energetic. Must be the caffeine, I thought (Coke has much more caffeine than coffee). I allowed myself a can each day.

By spring, I was still rationing Diet Coke. I was sailing *Anne Marie 2* with Yvonne and noticed I could make it to five P.M., but then I needed my caffeine fix. It was just like alcohol and slippery food choices of decades earlier. If I had a little, the addiction returned.

Back home in Minnesota and Wisconsin, I made the rounds of our SSG stores. At each one, I'd fill up my "big gulp" cup with more Diet Coke. I could not stop drinking it, nor could I get enough. In a typical work day, I'd consume twelve to fifteen cans.

My therapist suggested that I cut down to two cans a day. For an addict, there is no such thing. Moderation is not in our vocabulary.

As the days passed, my consumption increased. Finally, I was driving Interstate 94 to Hudson and I thought, "I'm going to get stopped for drunk driving." I was so high on caffeine that I couldn't concentrate. I was completely out of touch with my senses and close to a black out. That's how sinister addiction can be.

In less than twelve months, my addiction had returned in a gale force. I talked about this at my OA meetings, and I was scared. Caffeine could have been a lethal trigger leading me back to compulsive overeating and my other old addictions.

At home in St. Paul, I had a whole day alone. I took my recovery and meditation books with me out to the swimming pool in our backyard. I sat there for hours reading, thinking, and praying. I made it to five P.M. and into the evening without Diet Coke. Before going to sleep, I prayed that my obsession with caffeine would be lifted.

When I woke up, the obsession was gone.

My addictions are cunning, powerful, and patient. But I have a line of defense: the tools of recovery. I only have to use them.

NOTHING HAPPENS BY MISTAKE

My children's lives make me thankful I have a 12-Step recovery program: it is my "architecture" for living. I call on Steps One, Two, and Three of my program because they tell me that life will be unmanageable at times, I can find sanity, even in chaos, and I can turn my troubles and fears over to the God of my understanding. I have often wondered if Steps One, Two, and Three were created expressly for parents.

It's tough to realize that your span of control legally ends when children reach eighteen. As parents, I think we learn how *not* to be the center of the universe. I can love my children and worry about their choices for a lifetime, but they must live their own lives.

As some of my children have struggled, I've learned much more about practicing acceptance. Even with nearly three decades in recovery, I don't do this perfectly. Acceptance flies in the face of my need to control. With time, I have come to see the wisdom of acceptance. It is not about giving in, as I first thought. It is about living life on life's terms. Seeing reality. Knowing where I begin and end. Especially where my influence and control ends.

This is one of my favorite passages from the "Big Book" (*Alcoholics Anonymous: Big Book*, Fourth Edition, Alcoholics Anonymous World Services, Inc., 2001):

And acceptance is the answer to all my problems today. When I am disturbed, it is because I find some person, place, thing or situation—some fact of my life—unacceptable to me, and I can find no serenity until I accept that person, place, thing or situation as being exactly the way it is supposed to be at this moment.

Nothing, absolutely nothing happens in God's world by mistake. Until I could accept my alcoholism, I could not stay sober; unless I accept life completely on life's terms, I cannot be happy. I need to concentrate not so much on what needs to be changed in the world as on what needs to be changed in me and in my attitudes.

Inside every addict is a codependent. That's someone who believes he has a right and responsibility to make the lives of the people he loves better. Nevermind what a loved one wants, needs, or believes. Flaming codependents like me have all the answers, and we resent the hell out of people who reject our help. When we don't get our way, we are usually resentful, anxiety-ridden, self-righteous, and long-suffering. We play the victims, and it's ugly.

That's what Al-Anon is for: people who believe they can play God with other people's lives. Some people don't think this joke is one bit funny, but I do. Mark Lundholm is a nationally known comic who focuses on the fears, flaws, and foibles of recovering people and the people who love them. He knows what he's talking about because he's a recovering addict, himself. Lundholm says that Al-Anon is the only place in the world where "wine" is a verb.

I could have used more Al-Anon meetings when Anne Marie turned fifteen and began experimenting with drugs and alcohol at school. At the same time, I was afraid our Nordstrand family disease, depression, had begun to affect her. Within four years, Anne Marie was riding the crest of calamity and I tried too hard to monitor her movements, intervene, and protect her.

When she turned eighteen, Anne Marie decided to leave home without telling us where she was going. It lasted only two days, but I was a wreck. I tried to "push the river" by getting her into counseling. There were days when Anne Marie seemed depressed. That scared me, and Anne Marie's mom, Syble, had the same concerns. It was the first time Syble and I really worked together as a team, but I still lost my perspective. I was so worried about Anne Marie that my life became unmanageable. I forgot the principles of my recovery program and failed to turn the outcome over to my God. Anne Marie tells me I take on other people's pain. She's right.

I didn't accept Anne Marie's struggle; instead, I made it my own. I was convinced I could fix her. That never worked with my wives, why did I think it would work with my daughter? Insanity, a sage once said, is doing the same thing over and over again and expecting different results.

Anne Marie made it through her hard time. While in counseling, she heard plenty of horror stories about drugs and alcohol ruining people's lives. She resolved not to be one of those people. Anne Marie graduated with honors from San Francisco University and went on to the Hastings College of Law in San Francisco where she earned her law degree at age twenty-eight. After passing the California State bar, she landed a job with a firm in San Francisco, even in midst of the United States' economic crisis in 2009.

She's a success story; she is my heroine.

Just like John and Jennie.

As they faced dark times in their lives, I've struggled with my need to "fix" their problems and spare them pain. I know it's impossible and unwise to try.

John's hearing impairment from infancy sometimes made growing up and fitting in heartbreaking. He became resilient, and he is a fighter. He told me how he got around a tough part of Washington, D.C., where he attended the nation's best school for the hearing-impaired, Gallaudet University. John went to Gallaudet after attending good schools in Minnesota where he was taught in grade school how to speak English and, in a special high school program, how to sign. His excellent education gave him the tools he needed to live in a hearing world and interact with his hearing-impaired and hearing friends.

John said he rode his bike through dangerous neighborhoods with a five-dollar bill in his pocket and another five-dollar bill hidden in his tennis shoe. "If someone rolls me, Dad," he told me, "I'll still have the money in my shoe."

My son is ambitious and has sometimes been a risk-taker. He and his cousin built their own skateboard park and went to San Diego for skateboard competitions. He played hockey for AHIHA (American Hearing Impaired Hockey Association) and earned a spot on the U.S. Deaf Olympics Hockey Team. They reached the finals and played Russia. John became an accomplished barefoot water skier. He became and remains an elite snow skier and dirt bike racer in Vail. He skis the most dangerous back bowls of Vail where avalanche threats are not uncommon.

John's wife, Tammy, who was hearing-impaired from an early age, worries about his aggressive approach to extreme sports. After all, they are raising three children together. An athlete herself, Tammy has learned to accept John's choices, believing that his experience, stamina, and highly developed senses will keep him out of harm's way. Tammy has helped me learn to accept John's life of high-risk sports.

When John phoned me and said his skiing partner died in an avalanche on the slopes the day before and John had chosen a different route down the same mountain, I swallowed my urge to lecture. Sure, he takes precautions. Yes, he travels with safety gear. "Trust me, Dad," he says, "I can read those mountains."

John's other senses have stepped in where his hearing has failed him. I still worry about him, but when I do, I remember the Serenity Prayer: "God grant me the serenity to accept the things I cannot change, courage to change the things I can, and the wisdom to know the difference."

My daughter Jennie met her future husband when she attended the University of Wisconsin at Madison. I took her to campus for freshman year and felt helpless when I saw the drunks and derelicts on State Street in downtown Madison; I could no longer protect her.

After graduation, she married Matt, who was just starting law school. They moved to St. Paul and began building a family of four rambunctious, athletic sons. Jennie earned her master's degree as a pediatric nurse practitioner; she worked in private practice and joined the St. Paul Schools. When their boys were ages six to fifteen, Jennie and Matt ended their marriage. Jennie forged a relationship with her best friend, Jane, and we gained another grandson, Gabe.

I struggled to understand the transformations in our family. There was nothing I could do to change the outcome. All I could do was love my daughter, love Jane, and love my son-in-law Matt. I learned to listen to Jennie and accept her truth about what makes her happy. Sometimes I have a hard time hearing people—really taking what they say to heart. I felt great anxiety during that time. When I was out of control, Matt says I was like my old friend Barkley. He curled in the corner, chewing his paw. I "chew" on things that aren't my business for far too long.

After they parted, Jennie remained in their St. Paul home and Matt moved into our basement for five weeks. My relationship with him was so important to me, and I didn't want to lose it. Jennie was always supportive of my relationship with Matt and, to her great credit, remains so. Matt and I disagreed about how some things should evolve as his marriage ended. My controlling nature kicked in. Matt and I butted heads with our strong convictions. It was rugged, but ultimately, we managed to preserve the love, respect, and regard between us.

Matt told me I had the greatest impact on him when I was willing to be vulnerable and humble. I described my failed marriages and my sadness when the track dream died. I talked about what it was like growing up on a farm in Ellsworth, believing I was the only flawed kid in a pack of high-achieving siblings.

By sharing our lives, we could see beyond our immediate pain. We had a glimpse of the bigger picture—the one that God designed for each of us.

Matt sent me a card not long after he and Jennie began their heart-breaking ending, and Matt examined his life and future. It was a black card with white letters. Stark and plain, it said simply, "Barn's burnt down...Now I can see the moon."

As Anne Marie, Jennie, John, and Matt struggled, I faced some of my old demons again. They helped me grow up. This passage from a daily meditation in *For Today*, (OA, Inc., 1982) summarizes my evolution, thanks to them:

Beliefs I was so sure about have turned out to be wrong. Foremost among them is the idea that if I take complete charge of my life, asking no help from any quarter, things will turn out the way I want them.

But it never has happened that way. Only when I give up being in charge, will peace of mind enter my life.

All my progress toward sanity and balance comes from this one, magnificent change.

NINE

A 'SQUEAKY CLEAN' LIFE HAS ITS BENEFITS

LIFE IS MAGICAL

Mid-morning: Yvonne and I were sipping coffee in the cockpit of *Serenity*. "Monty," our autopilot, was holding the course of 180 degrees magnetic from St. Lucia to St. Vincent. The winds were tropical soft at fifteen knots out of the east. The sun was bright. Not a cloud. The sea was perfectly flat as our sailboat sliced through the turquoise water. Magical.

We had said a final good-bye to my ninety-seven-year-old mother a few days before in Hudson, Wisconsin, with the whole Nordstrand family gathered to honor their "Gram." Her huge heart finally gave out.

I'm told that mail, even from people who aren't part of our family, addressed simply to "Gram" at the Hudson Post Office easily found its way to her door.

She wrote countless letters, too. When my nephew Scott lived in Alaska and held a senior position in government, he had a running account detailing the news of family members and Gram's thoughts about his life. He said it was like his diary, only he didn't write it.

Gram had grit—the little girl raised on a Nebraska ranch who trained her own pony. She was a brave little six-year-old when her mother died. At sixteen, she worked ten hours a day at a Woolworth's in Chicago where she was promoted to head cashier. When my mother married Dad, they moved to Ellsworth, Wisconsin, to learn farming. She even raised five hundred chicks and drove a horse and buggy five miles to town to sell her eggs. Gram's first son died, and she lived with my father's debilitating depression. She propped up Dad and spread around her love by making huge meals for family and friends, even strangers.

For Gram, food was love. For me, food became the enemy. How could she ever understand the power that food had over me?

The sun sparkled on *Serenity's* deck. Then I saw the first, glistening dorsal fin, then another. A whole pod of dolphins broke the surface. They darted and dove in chaotic joy. They multiplied until the water around *Serenity's* hull was boiling with nimble, gunmetal gray bodies rolling and playing. Dolphins are often attracted to boat hulls. They believe we're fellow fish in this vast ocean. This morning's aquatic escort was different. We often saw twenty or thirty dancing on our bow. This morning there were hundreds, maybe a thousand, dolphins. They were on all sides of us, as far as we could see.

I like to think that I was seeing Gram's spirit—as big as the ocean—present in those dolphins, reminding me that she is still just as present in my life as God.

LIVING WITH THE ENEMY

I had twenty-eight years in recovery from compulsive overeating in 2010, but food is still my enemy. I am amazed when I come home from enjoying a satisfying, healthy meal with Yvonne and I still want a bag of chips, a big handful of peanuts, or other salty, fatty foods. If I'm at a social event with a buffet table laden with dangerous foods, my addict brain tells me I can have a taste. I've seen it play out: if I give in, I'll have a small portion, then I'll start sneaking more.

My chronic illness will not go away. In the same way that an alcoholic can't drink in moderation, I can't eat my "binge foods" in moderation, either. Once an alcoholic begins drinking again, he doesn't know when he will stop. I have the same experience. If I give in to the "sexy" or "exciting" foods on my binge list, I'm powerless. Sugar is a stimulant, so is caffeine. Foods made with white flour, fat, and salt are my drugs. If I abuse them I'm going to feel high, out of control, and anxious. When my abuse finally ends, I have a physical hangover and I'm swimming in shame, depression, and fear. My only defense is to resist acting on my cravings that are sometimes just as powerful as they were thirty years ago.

Here's the good news: each time I abstain, my recovery gets stronger and I feel healthier, more centered, and satisfied with my life. I know that my disease is progressive but so is my recovery.

I still have slips from my "squeaky clean" eating, but they aren't week-long binges anymore. They are shorter in duration and longer in between—sometimes years. There is no such thing as perfect adherence to a food plan in OA. Slips are part of recovery because we're faced with food choices daily. At least alcoholics can keep booze out of their lives.

One of my friends with lots of years in the program skipped breakfast and lunch on a recent business trip. He binged on Cinnabons at the airport. Drawn by the fragrant aroma, he got so high on sugar, he missed his plane. He's a smart, responsible, can-do guy, but his disease took over. It could easily have been me.

As long as I'm willing and remain teachable, a slip is a setback; but it's something I can turn around. Today, when I have a slip only an hour or, at most, a day passes before I ask my sponsor for help, pray, write out my food plan, and get back to the basics of my program.

TRACING A SNEAKY DISEASE

None of us in Overeaters Anonymous will ever recover from compulsive overeating. The monster is always inside, and it can be triggered by emotional slips, as well as physical slips. I have to be on guard because my sneaky disease can rationalize anything.

I keep food journals, especially when I'm feeling stressed, out of control, or vulnerable. When I'm traveling and my routine changes, I'm on shaky ground, too. The journals offer simple proof of what it's like to live with the enemy:

"Arrived in Florida with all the kids. Had bad night with food. Another example of once I take that extra bite, my life is out of control."

"Father's Day. Doing OK with food. Jennie, Nick, and Sam went home this A.M. Yvonne is still upset about a disagreement we had last night. I know we always work it out. I will NOT let it affect my food choices."

"Wednesday, June 13: Did a lot of exercise in A.M.—weights, Pilates, swim. Had OK day. Healthy dinner, but then got into the fruit bowl of blueberries and topped them off with Grape-Nuts. Kept going with just Grape-Nuts and milk. Several small bowls. Felt bloated. Slept poorly and had bad dreams. I'm disgusted. I have to turn my life and food choices over to God...before I pick up that extra helping."

"Best Sunday BBQ ever. No white flour. No bread or potatoes. Nixing white flour is my answer to extra stress of demands in Minnesota. Perfect weather helps, too."

"Tuesday before going to Mayo. ½ PowerBar, small bowl cereal after workout. Lunch and dinner: no carbs, only protein and veggies. Apple before bed. GREAT NEWS from Mayo. PSA test is good."

Reviewing my journals gives me evidence of how my mental state affects my food choices. If I summarize this relationship in a simple statement, it is this: when I am living in my addiction, I am driven by fear and self-loathing, so I use food to feel better. When I choose recovery, I live in love. Love for myself, love for Yvonne, and love for everyone around me. I choose my foods with care.

When I follow my plan and try to do the "next right thing" in every aspect of my life, I'm happy, joyous, and free. I know who I'll be tomorrow, two weeks from now, two years from now. I can plan trips, take reasonable risks in my business life, step outside my comfort zone, and try new things. Squeaky clean eating isn't a penance; I love my meals, and life is easy. I love the social aspect of being present with my family and friends. That's the great gift of living in recovery—love, not fear.

I can face the unexpected with more serenity, too, even in 2005 when I was diagnosed with glaucoma and prostate cancer, even in 2008 during the United States' economic freefall. I know I am not in control.

TAKING MY INVENTORY DAILY

This program requires me to live in gratitude and acceptance, and it does not allow me the luxury of holding resentments or trying to exert too much control over people and life's events.

This recent, daily reading (*Today's Gift*, Hazelden Foundation, 2009) described my issue with total accuracy:

Let's cut right to the heart of the matter: We get in trouble if we try to run our own lives. Our ego starts to mess things up. We try to control things we can't control. We think we're smarter than we are. We think we can run things just fine by ourselves. What's the end result? We end up alone—spiritually and sometimes physically—and in trouble.

That's where Step Ten of my 12-Step program comes in.

In Steps One through Three, I admitted I was powerless over food and that a Higher Power (I call that power God) could return me to sane eating and living. I began to turn my life and my will over to the care of God, as I understood God, twenty-eight years ago. At the beginning, especially for a control freak like me, that was often an hourly decision. Sometimes every ten minutes!

In Steps Four through Seven, I took an honest, thorough look at myself: my assets and my liabilities. My liabilities—we call them "defects of character"—are my stumbling blocks. These are my fears and behaviors that get in the way of being happy, sane, and loving to myself and others. Every day, I humbly ask God to remove these defects and I do my part by working a healthy recovery program.

In Steps Eight and Nine, I examined how I hurt others and I made amends to those people, asking nothing in return. Sometimes I made amends in person, sometimes in a letter, sometimes in what we call "living amends"—changing my behavior, especially toward the person I hurt.

The Tenth Step asks me to continue taking my "personal inventory" and, when I'm wrong, promptly admit it. We call this a "maintenance step" in recovery because Steps One through Nine prepared me by recognizing my powerlessness over food, turning to a Higher Power for help, facing the pain I caused for others (and myself), asking God to remove my defects of character, and making amends to the people I hurt.

If I find myself upset with Yvonne, Kathy, Gail, or others, I quickly realize that the only constant here is me. I review Step Ten. Now, the Tenth Step keeps me on track, every day. I'm more alert to my defects when they resurface. When they do, I notice them sooner. Maybe I just take a deep breath and reflect on what I've just done or said. Maybe I say a silent prayer. If I'm really struggling, I call my recovery sponsor for feedback. If my devil dance with an old defect has hurt someone else, I make amends as soon as I can because the longer I wait, the worse it feels. And what a relief it is to honestly "own my part."

Some of us take our personal inventory as the day progresses in a kind of "spot check." Some review the day at bedtime. Still others jot notes in a journal. If I'm brooding about something and I'm fearful, anxious, angry, or resentful, I have learned to turn my will and my life over to the care of God. It's not about abdicating my personal responsibility, but it *is* about delegating the outcome to a power greater than I am. My job is to act out of love, not fear. That's easy to say, often hard to do. Without God's help, it would be impossible.

I DON'T FLY SOLO

There are two more Steps in my 12-Step program, and they are life savers. One is my "guidance system," and the second defines how I show up in the world each day.

I believe that successful, lifetime recovery from any addiction requires a healthy and active spiritual component. Without God's intervention in my life, I would still be abusing food or, worse, I'd be dead. Remember, I tried everything: diet pills, diets programs of all kinds (even some healthy ones), "controlled eating," steely willpower. Every time, my efforts ended in uncontrolled eating, shame, and fear. I have a mental and physical obsession with food. I use food to fill the "hole in my soul" when I'm flying solo without God's guidance system.

Millions of people in recovery from addictions of all kinds believe they are being healed by a power greater than themselves. They are convinced that continued recovery depends on a strong spiritual program—however they define it. For some, that Higher Power is God, for others it's nature, and for still others, it's their 12-Step recovery group.

At the heart of spirituality in recovery is this key realization: regardless of how I define god, I am *not* God.

Remember, I was a kid who stole coins out of the church collection plate and my dad warned me about the excesses of organized religion. I'm not a regular church-goer, but I check in with my God every day. That's Step Eleven. Here's how it reads: "Sought through prayer and meditation to improve our conscious contact with God, *as we understood Him*, praying only for knowledge of His will for us and the power to carry that out."

Notice the italicized part. This 12-Step program has a lot of latitude (many recovering women have taken the gender reference out). You decide who your God is. I did.

"Conscious contact" is crucial because God's feedback is my daily guidance system. When I pray, I ask God for help. When I meditate, shut my mouth and listen, that's when I remain open. I begin to understand what God's will is for me. Here's the tricky part: I have to suspend what I *think* God is going to tell me and wait for the *real* answer. I can't command it. I have to wait for it and trust the process.

When I do that, honestly and humbly, I have never been disappointed. Answers often come to me in my own instincts or thoughts. They come through other people and appear in my daily readings, too. Often, my readings speak so directly to me, that they seem to have everything in them but my name. That's conscious contact. My commitment is to be conscious and alert. I reach out to my God regularly, just as I would make frequent contact with a treasured friend.

Step Twelve is the bonus Step. Here's how it reads: "Having had a spiritual awakening as a result of these Steps, we tried to carry this message to compulsive overeaters and to practice these principles in all our affairs."

I never saw a burning bush. My "spiritual awakening" seeped into me. The more I put God in the front seat of my imaginary two-seater bicycle, the better I started to feel. The more I relied on God's guidance system, the better choices I made. I learned to trust this power greater than myself and I awakened. I believe I am living the life God always intended for me and I'm becoming the person He had in mind all along.

Philosopher and author Joseph Campbell said, "The privilege of a lifetime is being who you are." Recovery gives me that.

When people awaken to recovery, we want to carry the message to others. That's the reason I wrote this book. Some people choose to remain anonymous, and that is their right. They carry the message in quiet service to others. I've chosen a different path. By telling you what my life was like, how it changed, and what life is like now, I hope my story will help you or a loved one.

Step Twelve calls me to live the principles of the 12 Steps: honesty, openness, willingness, service, and humility. These Steps are the best "architecture for living" I've ever come across. Their fundamentals are reflected in all the world's major religions and in the teachings of the most respected philosophers: Buddha, Mohammed, and Jesus. I don't do it perfectly, but I try to live these principles daily.

A MIRACLE WALKING (...BIKING, CLIMBING, SAILING, AND SKIING)

What is my life like today? I feel like a miracle walking.

I am more physically fit and stronger than I've ever been. I engage in sports that challenge people half my age. I've maintained a healthy weight for nearly thirty years, and I lost that weight only once. I maintain my weight by sticking to a simple, "squeaky clean" eating plan—one day at a time. My setbacks with prostate cancer and glaucoma are manageable. My food slips are short, and I'm not too proud to ask for help.

I have learned how to be fully present in intimate relationships with my wife, my children, their partners, and grandchildren. When Yvonne and I married, there was a lot of talk about "blended families." I thought it was a therapist's term that didn't happen in real life. Together, Yvonne and I have five children and none of them are genetically related. One is Yvonne's biological child and one is my biological child. Our other three children are adopted. I like to tell people that we have five grown children and three are adopted…but I can't remember which three.

We have eight grandchildren. Six are boys between six and seventeen, and they are all superb athletes, especially in soccer, skiing, and hockey. Our two little girls are infants, and we delight in spoiling them. Yvonne and I believe that grandchildren are God's way of giving parents a second chance. Both of us struggled with parenting in our younger years. Yvonne was going through her divorce, and I had multiple addictions ruling my life. When I used food, alcohol, speed, caffeine, gambling, or work, it was impossible to be in a complete relationship with my children.

Yvonne's daughter Katie remembers how significant our first grandchild, Nicholas Burton, was to strengthening our "merged family." Jennie and Matt announced they were pregnant the same day Yvonne and I married. When Nick arrived, Katie says his presence gave our family a new and unifying focus. All of us loved Nick, and we looked for even more opportunities to be together.

Katie and her husband, Rob, gave our family our first granddaughter, and I have made a surprising discovery: the more grandchildren I have, the more I am capable of loving. The unconditional trust and love between grandparents and grandchildren is unmatched.

Yvonne and I travel many weeks each year to our homes in Florida and Vail, to our sailing boat in the Caribbean, and back to St. Paul. Some of our favorite trips are family trips. A very special time for me is when a grandchild reaches age five I personally take him to Disney World. We travel first class, starting with the limo trip from Orlando airport, our suite on the concierge floor of the Contemporary Hotel, and a two-day Disney World ticket. We swim in the hotel pool, ride the monorail to the Disney Park, and watch daily fireworks from our balcony. When they are with Grandpa, they can do anything they want, including eating crackers in bed! I've taken all six of our boys on that exact trip, and I can't wait until our next grandchild reaches the magic "five" mark so I can take her to the Magic Kingdom, too.

In 1995, we took the entire Nordstrand family, including our two mothers, to the island of St. Croix in the U.S. Virgin Islands. On an inside passage cruise to Alaska in 2002, our family got so close to the glaciers that we could see and hear huge slabs of ice break and cascade into the ocean. Each year we have at least one Nordstrand family trip to our home in Florida. We spend our family winter holidays skiing together in Vail, and we often take a couple of grandchildren with their parents on one of our sailing trips to the Caribbean. I'm lucky that so many of my children and grandchildren love sports and the outdoors, as I do. Our son Brian, twenty-seven, for example, is a hockey coach for a semi-pro team. He's up for any challenge. Our son-in-law, Rob, includes Matt and me in a relay triathlon each year. Happily I'll always have willing playmates.

Yvonne and I also take one, major international trip each year, and our destinations in the past fifteen years mirror a map of the world: Paris, Beijing, Hong Kong, Vienna, Budapest, Hungary, Milan, Venice, Amsterdam, London, Singapore, Tokyo, Taipei, South Africa, Rome, Athens, Egypt, Israel, and Vietnam.

I am a fortunate man. My addictions no longer come between me and the people I love. I have learned that recovery is all about shifting from asking, "Hey, what about me?" to "Hey, what about them?"

I think of a friend, also a grandpa, who retired to a comfortable, leisurely life. What did his grandchildren remember of him after he died? Not much. They told me Grandpa mixed a lot of martinis, grilled steaks, and spent weekends at his cabin with his new, younger wife. It's a common story and a heartbreaking one.

NO LONGER BOXED IN

Though I'm out of town, I'm never out of touch. My team at SSG keeps me informed, and I can always respond to their queries quickly. I trust the people who work for me, and I've learned to surrender my old need to control and micromanage.

SSG remains a multi-million-dollar enterprise that employs over four hundred people and operates convenience stores and other businesses in Minnesota and Wisconsin. We've grown since our founding in 1971, largely because our people take pride in how they run and manage each store and they keep an eye out for expansion opportunities. Over time, I've been able to attract strong, talented people. I've given them responsibility and authority to act, and I've encouraged them to be creative. They have the freedom to do what they do best. In a very real sense, we encourage SSG people to be "*intrapreneurs*"— building their stores with the resources of our corporation backing them. The same is true for our real estate leasing and management company, Burt Nordstrand & Associates.

I trust my key colleagues and advisors because our relationships are long-term, often spanning twenty and thirty years. I feel great loyalty and gratitude to them, and I respect their professionalism and discipline. I recognize that I would not be blessed with these relationships if I was still living my addicted life.

Because all of these people are so capable and trustworthy, I am freed-up to focus my attention where I am most needed: in my business, my family, my recovery program, and my community.

I no longer live my life in "boxes" the way I did before recovery. I don't need to keep a tight lid on each "box" and limit what I let people see. My life today is a seamless whole. I have nothing to hide.

For me, recovery has to do with living from within, giving from within, and loving from within.

SURRENDERING MAGICAL THINKING

The promises of recovery assure us that our fears about financial insecurity will leave us. Growing up, my measure of worth was how much cash I had in my pocket and how cleverly I could manipulate a financial transaction in my favor. That was how I kept score. As I matured and got into business, I engaged in what people call "magical thinking." I fantasized about investing short or long in the market and turning one million into one hundred million dollars. I imagined what all that wealth would buy—yachts, private planes, megahomes. For a few years, I lived the high life and I obsessed about moneymaking schemes.

Before my recovery, I took lots of risks. I pushed as hard as I could, and I moved at warp speed. I was proud of my stamina, my control, and my penchant for perfection. My ego drove me to build more and more SSG stores. The "next big deal" attracted me. The excitement, the drama, and the gambles of entrepreneurial life thrilled me. When my success attracted attention, the recognition was a drug. The very qualities that defined me as an addict also made me a successful businessman. But my addictions were cutting my life short.

These days, rather than going out and searching for the latest profit-making idea, I'm more involved in giving back to my family and to society. The risks I take in business are measured. I don't crave the drama, and I don't need the recognition.

I don't obsess about money any longer; I didn't panic when the market plummeted or a project like the dog track wasn't the financial bonanza I thought it would be. Because of my recovery program, I do my part and turn the outcome over to God, believing that my financial life will evolve just as it was intended. Fear isn't driving my decisions. My job is to do the best I can. I am not responsible for the outcome.

Yvonne and I have established trusts for our children and grandchildren so they'll have a resource to tap and supplement their already productive lives. These trusts will make their lives easier and fund their educational aspirations. Yvonne and I are investing in their future dreams.

My goal is to teach my children and grandchildren the importance of having rewarding careers, taking responsibility for their personal growth, contributing to society, and having fun along the way. As I have.

Rather than build more wealth for wealth's sake, I have created the Burt Nordstrand Foundation, which will give financial support to programs for the hearing-impaired, chemical dependency treatment programs, and other health, arts, and educational endeavors. Just as the Twelfth Step of my recovery program tells me to "carry the message" of hope to other addicts, I am committed to giving, after a lifetime of striving and earning.

THE REAL MAGIC

I am a happy man, blessed in more ways than I ever imagined possible.

That sad, fearful little boy from an Ellsworth, Wisconsin, farm has dropped his gunnysack full of fears, shame, and desperation. That little boy didn't believe he was lovable; the grown-up boy knows he is. My recovery has changed me from the inside out.

C.S. Lewis once said that in our adversity, God shouts to us. God shouted to me when I hit my addicted "bottom" in the early 1980s. An addict reaches his bottom when he stops digging.

When I stopped digging and asked for help, God lifted my obsession with compulsive overeating. He gave me a chance to heal. I do my footwork every day to stay grounded, especially when my old demons re-visit me. I am connected and guided by a power greater than myself. Today, I am convinced that recovery is stronger than addiction because I see it enduring in my life and in the lives of countless others. Recovery is the triumph of love over fear.

Love is the singular, eternal force that gives meaning and hope to my life.

EPILOGUE

We are anchored off the coast of Antigua, home of some of the world's most beautiful beaches. We are in Crocus Bay, the sun has just set and the sky is a palette of reds, pinks, and oranges. There is not a single boat, or a light, in sight.

Yvonne and I share our hammock on the bow of *Serenity*.

Pelicans dive for their dinner from the high cliffs as we wait for the full moon to rise.

Life is good.

APPENDIX A

THE TWELVE STEPS OF ALCOHOLICS ANONYMOUS

(Alcoholics Anonymous: Big Book, Fourth Edition, Alcoholics Anonymous World Services, Inc., 2001)

1. We admitted we were powerless over alcohol—that our lives had become unmanageable.

2. Came to believe that a Power greater than ourselves could restore us to sanity.

3. Made a decision to turn our will and our lives over to the care of God as we understood Him.

4. Made a searching and fearless moral inventory of ourselves.

5. Admitted to God, to ourselves, and to another human being the exact nature of our wrongs.

6. Were entirely ready to have God remove all these defects of character.

7. Humbly asked Him to remove our shortcomings.

8.   Made a list of all persons we had harmed, and became willing to make amends to them all.

9.   Made direct amends to such people wherever possible, except when to do so would injure them or others.

10. Continued to take personal inventory and when we were wrong promptly admitted it.

11. Sought through prayer and meditation to improve our conscious contact with God, as we understood Him, praying only for knowledge of His will for us and the power to carry that out.

12. Having had a spiritual awakening as the result of these Steps, we tried to carry this message to alcoholics, and to practice these principles in all our affairs.

APPENDIX B

THE TWELVE STEPS OF OVEREATERS ANONYMOUS

(Overeaters Anonymous, Overeaters Anonymous, Inc., 1980)

1. We admitted we were powerless over food—that our lives had become unmanageable.

2. Came to believe that a Power greater than ourselves could restore us to sanity.

3. Made a decision to turn our will and our lives over to the care of God as we understood Him.

4. Made a searching and fearless moral inventory of ourselves.

5. Admitted to God, to ourselves, and to another human being the exact nature of our wrongs.

6. Were entirely ready to have God remove all these defects of character.

7. Humbly asked Him to remove our shortcomings.

8. Made a list of all persons we had harmed, and became willing to make amends to them all.

9. Made direct amends to such people wherever possible, except when to do so would injure them or others.

10. Continued to take personal inventory and when we were wrong promptly admitted it.

11. Sought through prayer and meditation to improve our conscious contact with God, as we understood Him, praying only for knowledge of His will for us and the power to carry that out.

12. Having had a spiritual awakening as the result of these Steps, we tried to carry this message to compulsive eaters, and to practice these principles in all our affairs.

ABOUT THE AUTHORS

Carol Pine has been a professional writer and business journalist for thirty-five years. She has written twenty-seven books and authored prize-winning business columns for the *Saint Paul Pioneer Press* newspaper and *Corporate Report* magazine. For fifteen years she served as an adjunct professor at the University of Minnesota School of Journalism and Mass Communications.

Burt Nordstrand has been in recovery from compulsive overeating for thirty years. While struggling with food and other dangerous addictions, he started SSG Corporation in 1971 and transformed the gas-and-convenience-store industry. As of 2010, Nordstrand's multimillion-dollar company employs five hundred people in forty locations in Minnesota and Wisconsin. Along with his successful ventures in real estate development, Nordstrand is also an athlete and avid sailor. He and his wife, Yvonne, divide their time between Wisconsin, Minnesota, Colorado, Florida and the Caribbean. The couple has five children and eight grandchildren. They are active in philanthropy and in the recovery community through the Burt Nordstrand Family Fund.